*"Education
is the most powerful weapon
which you can use to change the world"
Nelson Mandela*

# Content

Part I ........................................................................ 4
    Introduction: .......................................................... 5
    1. Norway ............................................................. 12
    2. Australia: ......................................................... 19
    3. Switzerland ....................................................... 25
    4. Germany ........................................................... 32
    5. Singapore ......................................................... 40
    6. Denmark ........................................................... 48
    7. Ireland ........................................................... 56
    8. Canada ............................................................ 64
    9. South Korea ....................................................... 72
    10. Finland .......................................................... 81
    What do we do now .................................................... 89

Part II ..................................................................... 101
    How to overcome argentine finantial crisis? .......................... 102
    Can education explain argentine recurrent crises? .................... 109
    Does the voucher system in Sweden work? .............................. 117
    Five alternatives for preventing teachers' strike .................... 124
    Economic cycle in Argentina .......................................... 132

(or: "Why is there an economic crisis every 10 years in argentina?) ................................................................................... 132

Fibonacci taxation ................................................................. 138

Bibliography ............................................................................ 145

Index......................................................................................... 165

# Part I

## Introduction:

There is currently a large amount of information summarized in many indicators that cover the most varied statistics at a global level, highlighting one nation or another depending on the organization or author's point of views. However, we don't have comprehensive studies telling us about this countries' background, recognizing them as a result of historical events, with complex causes that affected each nation's culture and their people's identity. By contrasting just figures or percentages, we forget their roots. The organizations responsible for the publication of interrelated indicators (such as the OECD), focus their attention on the present and the possible outcome, but they rarely provide us with a context or historical framework necessary to understand what lies behind the evolution of certain policies that effect, at the end of the day, the welfare of a nation. And without this context, the only way to interpret the information is given by each person or cultural paradigms. Or by historical references that are now probably outdated, or disconnected from the historical events that took place to give a sense to the current situation of a given geography. We hear for instance that in Singapore the State provides prime quality health care to its citizens for a fraction of US budget, or that in Nordic countries there is an extensive welfare system. We read a specialized magazine that highlights Nordic countries as "socialist" and at the same time another article highlights them as paladins of free markets. But to what extent is it useful to identify such isolated characteristics? The analysis of a country is a complex framework of historical events, cultural points of view, local beliefs and circumstances, both political and economic. Such complexity requires contextualizing these stories within a comprehensive analysis. Each story is a loose piece that invites us to assemble the jigsaw puzzle that each nation represents to be able to see the full picture. Bearing this in mind, we will address the task to figure out different socioeconomic models from a general point of view, considering their histories, idiosyncrasies, educational, health and tax systems and the commercial relationship with the world.

This book focuses on ten cases, and their choice has been *ad hoc* though closely related to the Human Development Index. As mentioned, being just a final number, it leaves aside each nation's history and background, but it is considered to be a more representative indicator than the GDP or GDP per capita, as it qualitatively measures a society through key dimensions of human development such as longevity, health, knowledge and the standard of living. These ten models are inspiring due to distinctive reasons: some are economies that historically managed to provide a high standard of living to their inhabitants, and they bring us worthwhile teachings; others are stories of completely unpredictable economic miracles that reveal us invaluable opportunities to apply to Latin America. There are countries from the most diverse latitudes, with surprisingly different idiosyncrasies, chosen in this way in order to combine similarities that can transcend a particular culture, a common history or analogous policies. Based on diversity, our interest is focused on discovering factors that manifest themselves unequivocally around the planet to recognize a pattern that explains what drives certain economies to success and condemns others to failure.

Before going into detail, there is a particular aspect, common to all societies, which is necessary to unravel from the beginning: education. More precisely, the reason why in Latin America private education institutes attract such a significant percentage of the population. The explanation has two main protagonists, the British/American influence and the influence of religion. Regarding the former, the British monarchy was the first champion of liberal ideology throughout the XIX century, arguing that government role should be reduced to a minimum expression, since individuals make better decisions about their destiny than governments. This school of thought obviously moved to all British colonies and especially to the new lands in the United States of America. Therefore, Latin America received a double dose of liberal doctrine, first with the political influence of the power British powerhouse who dominated the world during the nineteenth century and part of the twentieth century, and then Latin America went on to receive American influence (Puiggrós, 2015), with similar orientation. In all these territories, the tendency is to privatize and standardize education. Beyond the Channel, France experienced during the 18th century the surge of the Enlightenment, which advocated for reason, science and progress as superior sources of knowledge as opposed to faith. Education, until that time, was taught mainly in religious institutions and directed to a small elite. From the influence of John Locke and Jean Jacques Rousseau, intellectuals would start to visualize man as a member of society rather than a "God's son". Locke stimulated knowledge development beyond the Bible, promoting reading to cover the greatest amount of knowledge available, and to find reason in the common sense and experimentation. In the European Catholic territories, the Church and governments clashed for control of the educational monopoly, resulting in religious schools dedicated to the teaching of a wealthy minority and public schools covering the needs of the most disadvantaged classes to ensure their access to education. The government was forced to resort to the wide presence of the Church in each recess of its domains to reach children who were out of reach, giving rise to different degrees of social segregation depending on each country. In England, religious institutes continued to provide education to the elite leading to the privatization of education, and later they would spread throughout America in the form of privately managed teaching institutes, many of them settling in our region towards the end of the 19th century and the beginning of the 20th, and surviving until today.

It is worth examining the evolution of government responsibility in other regions. In the Protestant European territories, there was no conflict of the magnitude mentioned above after the Enlightenment. Frederick II the Great, King of Prussia from 1740 to 1786, laid the foundations for an educational system that would integrate the entire population in an inclusive manner. He ordered the construction of numerous establishments where religious education was given, but under the control of the kingdom. Later, there would be a transition to state control in the early nineteenth century, in an organized way. The State absorbed the Lutheran Church responsibility, consolidating their goal to educate the population, and both understood that knowledge is a tool for development and preservation. This pedagogical conception in unison is due to the marked importance of education in the ideas of Martin Luther. Education began to be offered to the population as a whole from the age of 5 to 13-14 years supervised by religious leaders but controlled at the government level by the authority. The German States then established a system of universal free education without distinction of classes that lasts until today, and that spread northward taking root as a social policy in the Scandinavian countries (Cubberley, Ellwood P., 1920).

Independence leaders throughout the southern cone of Latin America, meanwhile, were instructed primarily in Spain, and brought with them the ideas of reason as the fundamental basis of the new republics. The Latin American liberals and conservatives then fought, the first in pursuit of an educational responsibility in the hands of the central government and the second in favour of preserving a religious education. After a long confrontation due to the conflict of interests, the liberals managed to implement a system of national scope that allowed to fight against the high degree of illiteracy that dominated the continent, but this continued to coexist with religious education institutes because of the difficulty that represented to the blossoming nations to reach every corner of the territory, where there was no town without its parish, no matter how small or remote the village was.

Another parallel historical event would mark the fate of schooling in Latin America: the arrival of the Catholic religion. The year of the conquest of America by the Spaniards was also the year of the *Reconquista* of the south of the Iberian Peninsula by the crown, which ended eight hundred years of religious dispute. The Catholic faith occupied every inch of society and the priority when encountering a universe of new beliefs in the unknown continent was that of the evangelization of the original inhabitants. With time, they became the institutions where the children of merchants, officials, etc. would study. With the advent of the independence movement of South America, these institutions had a territorial advantage over the State by occupying the length and breadth of the land. Religious education had managed to conquer a central place in the formation of local wealthy classes and as in Catholic Europe, the Church achieved sufficient power to fight for the continuity of its pedagogical work as a supplement to state education. It is for these two reasons that we find so many traditional schools in Latin America that are religious institutions, British institutions, or both.

The twenty countries with the highest HDI (Human Development Index) according to the United Nations Development Program are the following - in bold those included in this work-:

| #   | Country        | IDH   |
|-----|----------------|-------|
| 1   | *Norway*       | *0.949* |
| 2   | *Australia*    | *0.939* |
|     | *Switzerland*  | *0.939* |
| 4   | *Germany*      | *0.926* |
| 5   | *Denmark*      | *0.925* |
|     | *Singapore*    | *0.925* |
| 7   | Neatherland    | 0.924 |
| 8   | *Ireland*      | *0.923* |
| 9   | Iceland        | 0.921 |
| 10  | *Canada*       | *0.920* |
|     | USA            | 0.920 |
| 12  | Hong Kong      | 0.917 |
| 13  | New Zealand    | 0.915 |
| 14  | Sweden         | 0.913 |
| 15  | Liechtenstein  | 0.912 |
| 16  | United Kingdom | 0.909 |
| 17  | Japan          | 0.903 |
| 18  | *South Korea*  | *0.901* |
| 19  | Israel         | 0.899 |
| 20  | Luxemburg      | 0.898 |
| (...) |              |       |
| 23  | *Finland*      | *0.895* |
| 45  | Argentina      | 0.827 |

# 1. NORWAY

Why does Norway show the highest Human Development Index?

Birthplace of the Viking nation that dominated the northern seas, their cultural heritage was a strong fishing industry that was revolutionized in the 1960s by the discovery of oil in the seabed. This late finding gave a vigorous boost to the country's economy in the 70s, generating an extraordinary surplus (IMF, 2019a). As for its policy, Norway lays its foundations in the Scandinavian model, inspired by a welfare state that provides health and free education to its 5.5 million inhabitants while promoting an open markets' economy.

The oil sector is responsible for approximately 9% of the labour supply, 12% of GDP, 13% of revenues to public exchequer and 37% of exports («Europe: Norway—The World Factbook—Central Intelligence Agency», 2019). It is the twenty-first country in terms of proven oil reserves and the eighth in terms of its natural gas reserves, a resource that exports to the European Union supplying a third of its total demand («Europe: Norway—The World Factbook—Central Intelligence Agency», 2019). Norway invests the collected taxes from the oil industry in the largest global sovereign fund, valued at more than $ 1 billion, from which it obtains an annual yield of 6.1% for their investments in companies, bonds and real estate dispersed in seventy-two countries around the world (Norges Bank, 2019). Its exploration in search of new hydrocarbons continues, focusing mainly on the Arctic region, a policy that produced harsh criticism from environmental organizations.

    The Nordic welfare state model differs through its members (Norway, Denmark, Sweden, Finland and Iceland) but can be recognized by its objectives: promote economic efficiency; provide its society with an inclusive development from an early age; and provide job opportunities by favoring the establishment of international capitals keen on investing in their countries. In social policy, the cornerstone of the model is universalism: this means that public policies include the entire population rather than focusing on a structurally needy social sector - in order to avoid stigmatization.

Education and healthcare are free of charge and world-class quality services for all the inhabitants of the nation. Healthcare as a universal right was developed in parallel with the late industrialization of the Nordic countries that recently gained strength in the middle of the 20th century. Previously, however, there was a collective consciousness about the importance of having a healthy population, founded on a conception of the significance that this aspect has in the creation of wealth.

Education reached all the inhabitants in a more smooth way: the Lutheran Church was responsible for ensuring the literacy of the population since the sixteenth century, but when the ideas of the Enlightenment reached Nordic territory, the responsibility of coordinating and centralizing it was undertaken by the State. The monarchs relied on local parishes and instituted a council of local authorities that included the priest and the students' parents. The importance of forming a trained population was paramount for the whole society, and so each citizen became entitled to receive primary education without there really being a competition between the Church and the State for the educational monopoly, as it did in other latitudes. The Lutheran Church continued to have a heavy influence in the curriculum and in the governing bodies, but the central government was now accountable for controlling and managing the education system. The Church became responsible for the daily administration of the institutions, and the State of financing and regulate them. Denmark took the first step in 1814 by introducing seven years of schooling, then Sweden in 1842, followed by Norway in 1848 and Finland in 1866 (Kuhnle, Stein, 2004).

However, the Nordic paradigm changes radically when it comes to doing business, since state interventionism decreases considerably and paves the way to promote the development of the private sector and international trade. Companies invest in order to make a profit, and society has a positive attitude towards this.

These companies are based here on the extraordinary productivity per person -measured as GDP growth over active workers' year after year-, highly trained human resources and the ease of establishing business relationships with the rest of the world. Norway is, according to the World Bank, the eighth easiest country to install a new business. It stands out for the ease of starting a new company, ease of obtaining construction permits, registering a property, protection for SMEs and simplicity to solve insolvency situations. In the index of economic freedom elaborated by "The Heritage Foundation", it occupies the sixth place between 47 countries of Europe, standing out for the opening of its markets, the level of government integrity and its fiscal surplus. As for the transparency perceived by the population, it is the second country with the lowest corruption perceived behind New Zealand and the country with the greatest freedom of expression for the press. Gender equality is deeply established, and most women are immersed in the workplace in an equal situation.

Norway extraordinarily blends the presence of the State to provide equal opportunities with an environment conducive to economic development fostered through open markets and investment incentives. It offers the best available human resources through a system that stimulates everyone to reach their full potential. Markets reward this highly skilled workforce with heavy investments and generous salaries. This benefits both the people, who have a high standard of living, and the government, who has a high return on investment in education through taxes.

Health is a national priority, occupying 9% of GDP, the highest per-capita expenditure of OECD member countries. Children under 16 do not pay any medical charges, expenses incurred during pregnancy are fully covered as well as hospitalizations for emergencies. Visits to the attending physician are required to obtain a subsequent referral to a specialist. Both the attending physician and the specialists are not free but are governed through a co-payment system, and from a certain maximum limit, an exemption can be requested, which occurs in cases of chronic or catastrophic diseases. The co-payment implies that the State is responsible for 66% of the cost of the medical consultation, and the patient covers the remaining 33% (in 2018, the cost of the visit to the clinical doctor was around 37 euros). The State takes care of its citizens *'from the cradle to the grave'*. This offers support for families as by taking responsibility for children, the elderly and the sick, it gives some flexibility to people who should otherwise take up an important part of their time and money to care for them.

This way, people can be employed with the peace of mind that their loved ones are well protected.

The Norwegian education system currently provides public education to 97% of students in primary school (21,000 students attend private institutions out of a total of 624,000). In secondary school (16 to 18 years of age), the State reaches 93% of young people. The graduation rate is 94%, while in vocational school, it is 75%. The balance of both educational branches' results in eight out of ten people completing school education, with practically identical percentages for both genders (Statistics Norway, 2016). In addition to attending ordinary schooling, about one million people benefit from adult education. The country achieved outstanding results with its educational system, which manages to attract and retain school-age children until the cycle is completed. To sustain this structure, it incurs an expense equivalent to 6% of GDP, a level that some countries in Latin America reached only in recent years.

Regarding trade, Norway encourages free trade of most of the goods and services that it exchanges with the world. However, it presents some barriers in sectors or issues that it considers strategic. This is how we can see a restriction on the entry of foreign capital to mining, fishing, maritime transport, air transport, oil exploitation and some agricultural and beef products. As for its relationship with the European Union, through two referendums (which took place in 1972 and 1994) the population refused to enter the economic union. Despite this, it prioritizes imports from the European Economic Area (EEA) except for the agronomic and fisheries' sector where it establishes import barriers. These barriers exist although the agricultural sector only represents 1.5% of GDP (Office of the United States Trade Representative, 2015).

    In conclusion, a marked tendency towards the care and development of children can be seen through a complete public health coverage that begins after pregnancy and continues during adolescence. At the same time, its educational system is highly inclusive, since it is a government priority to offer equal opportunities for all its inhabitants. This equality not only benefits all young people but also lays the foundation for a labour market full of opportunities for companies. Everyone involved wins: unemployment is only 4%, companies have highly qualified professionals and the State finances through taxes 55% of its budget, which in 2017 had a surplus of 4.5% (Ministry of Finance, Norway, 2018).

## 2. AUSTRALIA:

The legacy of Sir Robert Menzies

British colony since 1788, a monarchical democracy since 1901, in the post-war period after World War II, government implemented policies to promote European immigration in order to increase its small population. It was characterized from the mid-nineteenth to mid-twentieth century with the progress that came associated with the gold rush in the country, and during the 20th century Australia developed a mixed economy with mining always occupying a vital role, central core around which the rest of the economy grew. Currently, 70% of GDP is associated with service areas - tourism, education and financial services. Its exports of goods are mainly based on natural resources such as iron, coal, natural gas, gold, wool and wheat. Its main trading partners until the 1960s were Great Britain and the United States, but since then Asian countries have been occupying increasingly prominent places, and today the largest number of exchanges is concentrated in their relations with China, Japan, United States and South Korea (Department of Foreign Affairs and Trade, 2019).

The twentieth century was deeply marked by the government of Sir Robert Menzies, of liberal inclination, who ruled two years between 1939 and 1941 and sixteen years between 1949 and 1966. It marked the course of the country with its post-war pro-immigration policy and its concern for education. He identified with the working middle class and with "the forgotten". During his government, he subsidized the study of children of very humble origin, tripled public spending on education, increased teacher salaries and founded monitoring committees on the state of education. Subsequent governments maintained this liberal ideological tendency. Currently, it maintains an open-market policy with few regulations on imports of goods and services. This has increased productivity, stimulated growth and creating a more flexible and dynamic economy. The tax system is strongly progressive (dividing the rate applied according to income in five tranches of 0%, 10%, 20%, 30% and up to a cap of 45%) and centralized in the national government, who distributes the resources discretionally.

The twenty-three million people who occupy the island-continent live by its coasts. The northeast has large stretches of beaches that attract tourists from all over the world. Kangaroo land is known worldwide for its unique flora and fauna, since 80% of the species found here are endemic, that is, they do not exist in other latitudes of the globe.

Regarding health, it invests 9.5% of its GDP, barely above the average of the OECD member countries. The public health system covers the entire population with very good results, and around 50% of them has a supplementary private medical insurance to expand their medical coverage. The public program generally covers 100% of the general practitioner, 85% of the specialist - the rest is paid by the patient through a co-payment with an annual limit, hardly reached by the majority of the population, from which the government covers all expenses incurred-, hospitalization expenses and dental expenses from 12 to 17 years old.

Regarding trade, Australia promotes free trade with different trading partners. Until the 1980s, it had important barriers to protect its industry (such as in the automotive and textile sectors) but since then it has moved towards a more open economy that currently has free trade agreements with New Zealand, Association of Southeast Nations Asian, Chile, China, Hong Kong, India, Indonesia, Japan, Korea, Malaysia and recently the United States and Peru. This increased presence in the global market helped in the last five years to go from having a trade deficit to a surplus of 2 billion dollars. Australia has a barrier to audio-visual content, requesting certain quotas of local content in the cinema, on TV and on the radio. It also has strict control over foreign investments, which receive authorizations at its discretion.

Regarding education, it is mandatory until 17 years old. Two-thirds of the students attend public schools and one third do so in private institutions - well above the average in the rest of the OECD member countries. The average number of students per classroom remains lower in state schools. As for universities, there are forty public universities that receive 93% of higher-education students, two international and one private. Australia has high levels of schooling, high-school attainment and participation of children in early education. The percentage of students with a performance below the national average is lower than in other countries (OECD). Teachers are well-prepared and paid. However, the 2015 Program for International Student Assessment (PISA) and Trends in the International Study of Mathematics and Science (TIMSS) in the last twenty years shows that, on the one hand, Australian students perform at levels above OECD average, but on the other hand, its overall performance has stagnated or decreased since 2000. In addition, rural and indigenous populations have lower academic performance and less access to tertiary education than the national average. Significant differences in student performance can also be found on PISA tests for students from different states and Australian territories (Department of Foreign Affairs and Trade, 2019).

Regarding its financing, the OECD observes that the educational budget is not very transparent, and it is especially difficult to identify the destination of the funds, resulting in cases of very similar schools with very different resources. As of 2014, in accordance with the Australian Education Law, and to attack the aforementioned problems, the government finances all Australian schools without any discrimination, encouraging equity for all its inhabitants. The new system implies that funds are determined based on a School Resource Standard (SRS). For non-governmental schools, their base funds are discounted based on the ability of the school community to contribute to the cost of running their school. In addition, all schools receive supplementary funds that address specific needs that the State subsidizes, such as students from vulnerable socioeconomic levels, from Aboriginal communities, with low levels of English and students with disabilities. Similarly, small schools and those in remote areas receive additional help (OECD, 2015a).

In conclusion, Australia is a country that grew after the immigration of mainly European workers, relying on mining to boost the industrial and financial sector. Natural resources are the core pillar from which the economic system orbits, laying a solid commercial base that in recent decades complemented with an impulse to the areas of services that grew exponentially to contribute strongly to economic development. Health and education provide support to the population in all its strata, focusing on children, with a healthcare system that protects them and an educational system that provides equal opportunities. This allows more than 75% of students to finish high school. Consequently, the labour market is attractive to companies that require skilled labour.

# 3. Switzerland

The headquarters of global finances

This small country in central Europe with no access to the sea and with very few natural resources is a pioneer in terms of peace and democracy, making its historical neutrality the perfect context to host many international institutions such as the Red Cross, United Nations, WHO, WTO, between about two hundred organizations. To such an extent it took its neutrality that it joined as a full member of the United Nations only in 2002 and takes not part of the European Union because of the 2001 referendum that resulted in 77% of the votes against it. Despite this, it is part of the European Free Trade Association (EFTA), a small and balanced economic area shared with Norway, Iceland and Liechtenstein. During the two World Wars, Switzerland retained its historic neutral stance, thus avoiding the devastating consequences on its territory of the clashes of its neighbours. Then, in the post-war era, the banking sector grew exponentially, pushing the average annual GDP increase to the order of 5% between 1950 and 1970 (Gapminder Foundation, 2015). At the same time, it developed a strong manufacturing sector headed by the food industry (Nestlé), pharmaceutical industry (Novartis and Roche), construction (Holcim) and chemical industry. Equally important is the development of the tourism sector, profiting from the Alps as its historic cities.

Taxes in Switzerland deserve special attention. According to a worldwide trend, corporate income tax has been falling dissimilarly in each canton during the last decade - globally, the decline was 3% in the 2007-2017 period. More than 850 multinational companies are based in Switzerland, making it the country with the highest concentration of 'multinationals in the Fortune 500' ranking per capita. This concentration is explained by the economic stability offered by the country, the aforementioned and characteristic neutrality and of course, exceptional tax advantages. In other words, these 850 multinational companies revenues collected worldwide arrive through complicated tax triangulation to a country of a population of 8.5 million people. These organizations exert great pressure on the government to keep on being business friendly, threatening the possibility of relocating to more favourable destinations if this does not happen. This puts the entire economy at risk since only 2.96% of companies contribute 90% of corporate taxes and 3.55% of people on higher incomes (usually managers thereof) contribute with more than 50 % of taxes on natural persons (Deloitte, 2015; KPMG, 2016, 2019). The main challenge that faces the Swiss government nowadays, is an important international pressure to establish controls against money laundering. As for residents, the Swiss tax system is strongly progressive (PwC, 2019).

Highlights: the net profit of the mentioned 850 multinationals was divided (as in 2015), according to the following percentages:
- **9%** of business had a negative profit below -10%
- **10%** of business had a negative profit between -10% and 0%
- **28%** of business had a positive profit between 0% and 5%
- **24%** of business had a positive profit between 5% and 10%
- **22%** of business had a positive profit between 10% and 20%

- **7%** of business had a positive profit greater than 20%
  - From this information, it follows that:
    - 81% of business had profits.
    - When business asks for cost reduction, probably this demand comes from the 47% of business on a profit lower than 5%, but benefits from these policies are embraced by all companies.

For fifty years, Switzerland has maintained special regimes that reduce the tax burden of holdings (they enjoy tax exemption at the level of the Swiss cantons and have a reduction in the payment of both the federal tax and the tax on company assets) and the international headquarters (excluding taxes on profits generated abroad). As of 2007, the European Union began pressuring Switzerland to abolish this regulation by arguing unfair competition. To avoid being included in the category of tax haven for the EU, the government decided to reform its legislation on these controversial points with the initiative called 'Corporate Tax Reform III'.

In terms of health, the total expenditure is 12.4% of GDP, the highest of the OECD European member countries (OECD, 2019). It is the sum of 7.9% of public spending plus 4.5% of individual spending, the latter percentage being particularly the one that pushes the economic sacrifice of society well above average, placing it as the most expensive healthcare system in Europe. Despite the wide range of private providers, competition is not reflected in a decrease in costs. Switzerland imposes by law the obligation to have private basic medical insurance, on which health companies cannot make a profit or refuse any applicant since it is covered by the State at the canton level. If the cost of insurance exceeds 10% of a person's income, then the State subsidizes the difference. It covers consultations with the general practitioner, most specialists, prescribed remedies, some vaccines, some general examinations, specific studies in risk groups (e.g. mammography if there is a medical history), and costs during pregnancy and until the first months of the baby and, until the age of 18, it also covers both the dental plan and the glasses or contact lenses. For additional coverage, there are supplementary plans on which health companies can make a profit and vary greatly in price. The high-cost issue of its medical system is equivalently shared with the United States, both countries curiously leaving much of their health system in private hands (Health Consumer Powerhouse, 2015; The Commonwealth Fund, 2017).

The Swiss education system is predominantly public, with only 5% of students attending private schools. The quality of its education placed Switzerland ninth between sixty-five OECD countries in the 2012 PISA tests. Its system is fully decentralized since each of the twenty-six cantons takes over its own jurisdiction, resulting in a flexibility than facilitates articulation to regional needs. Public spending occupies 5.1% of GDP on a sustained basis. In Switzerland, this is reflected in public schools with an average of 19 students per class in primary school, with a tendency in the last twenty years to increase classes with 13-16 students. While the percentage of children under 25 who finished high school in Switzerland in 2010 were 92.4%, in Argentina, for instance, those under 20 who finished high school in the same period were 39% -or 75%

if we consider only its capital city of Buenos Aires- (Swiss Coordination Centre for Research in Education, 2014).

Highlights of the 'Swiss Education Report':
- Students who attended kindergarten since age 3 earned 60 more points on the 2009 PISA tests than those who did not attend pre-school education. (Swiss Coordination Centre for Research in Education, 2014, p. 67)
- Attending pre-school at the age of three increases the opportunities for schooling for children from disadvantaged families since the interference of the family that, according to the report, adversely affects children's opportunities, is replaced to some extent for a quality educational program. (Swiss Coordination Centre for Research in Education, 2014, p. 77)
- From 1996 to 2010 the graduation rate of the upper secondary school for young people under 25 years varies between 90% and 94%. The objective of Switzerland is to bring it to 95%, without a deadline to meet this objective. (Swiss Coordination Centre for Research in Education, 2014, pp. 108-109)
- 90% of adults between 56 and 65 years old born in Switzerland completed high school, this tells us about the constant priority that education has been as a government policy. (Swiss Coordination Centre for Research in Education, 2014, p. 110)

Regarding trade, although it is a country with extremely open borders, it has strong restrictions on the importation of agricultural products. To these products, a tariff of 35.7% and a quota restriction are applied, while to the rest of the goods and services only a levy of 1.9% applies.

In summary, Switzerland consolidated its powerhouse position thanks to its advanced industry and its favourable business-friendly environment -in every possible way-. Given the shortage of natural resources, they concentrated on attracting international capitals to develop its economy, offering an extremely favourable context. Freedom is its banner in a range of aspects: cantons make a large number of autonomous decisions; it is a country very open to foreign trade except for the protection of its agricultural producers; and it has exceptionally flexible labour laws. Its educational system is at the forefront of Europe, and its health system covers the basic needs of its inhabitants. As we observed in the cases of Norway and Australia, they seem two fundamental elements for the development of a nation (90% of adults between 56 and 65 years completed high school, which speaks of a privileged position within the political agenda as early as the 1960s and before). This sounds logical, since a company needs skilled labour force and a healthy population in order to settle down, a variable that bring labour costs down, productivity upwards, and is an asset for Swiss society.

# 4. Germany

Wirtschaftswunder, or the "Miracle on the Rhine"

A prolific land in poets, writers and philosophers, Germany is an unequivocal synonym of precision and quality. It currently has 80 million inhabitants, the second most populous country in Europe after Russia. Reunited in 1990 after the fall of the Berlin Wall, the different regions vary significantly in idiosyncrasy, economy and geography. While the north is flat and fertile, the centre is an area of hills and the Bavarian Alps dominate the south, which is the most economically powerful («Europe: Germany—The World Factbook—Central Intelligence Agency», 2019). A third of the country is made up of forests, which prevented, to some extent, the advance of the Romans and together with the Rhine and Danube rivers marked the northern border of the Empire. Germany is famous for its exceptional engineers, 'made in Germany' is unquestionably synonymous with perfection: Volkswagen, BMW, Mercedes-Benz, Porsche, Audi, Telekom, Nivea, DHL, Bosch, Adidas, Puma, Allianz, Bayer, SAP, Siemens (among others) are world references in their respective fields. Angela Merkel was chosen eleven times by Forbes as the most powerful woman in the world.

The German territory suffered devastating consequences after World War II and faced a colossal challenge in unifying its two territories after the fall of the Berlin Wall. Its current situation as one of the most important economies in the world is a story of overcoming surprising adversities and obstacles. What happened from the post-war era to the present and how can a country devastated by the greatest global war conflict, become the leader of the European Union in just fifty years? The epic is commonly known as "the miracle of the Rhine River" (or "Wirtschaftswunder", literally "economic miracle"). Post-war West Germany was in ruins, shops broke daily and hyperinflation destroyed the currency. A quarter of the houses were demolished, and an additional quarter suffered significant damage. In the winter of 1948, Ludwing Erhard was appointed as minister of economy with the arduous task of rebuilding a nation from the ground up. Erhard was a promoter of "ordoliberalism": a model based on free-market capitalism combined with social policies that favoured competition between private funds, while guaranteeing its inhabitants a welfare state. In this way, it took away from Keynesian state interventionism prevalent in Britain, France and the United States, without neglecting the firm intention to protect the population and focusing on equal opportunities for all its inhabitants. Thus, the government instituted decent unemployment insurance, quality education for all children, sick work coverage, work accident insurance, disability insurance and retirement pension.

Erhard worried about eliminating the inherited price controls and production quotas in force in totalitarian Germany, since this practice consumed most of the authorities' time, on discussions about appropriate prices of goods and services, instead of finding ways out of the economic crises. He did so by issuing a radio announcement to the entire population without authorization from the allied inspectors. The American General Lucius Clay, responsible for the German transition immediately after the war, called him desperate after the announcements to say to him: "Mr. Erhard, my advisors tell me that you are making a terrible mistake." Erhard replied: "General, don't listen to them ... my advisors tell me the same thing" (Yergin, Daniel, 2002). The immediate consequences were swift, with a substantial increase in imports and an initial general price index increase, but thanks to the fact that the new Deutsche Mark laid its foundations in monetary stability; they fell to normalize in a span of one to two years. Industrial activity resumed its normal level, oriented towards the export of manufactures. At the same time, the government established by law, that large companies should secure a place in their directory for a union delegate so that workers' interests were represented in the most significant decisions. It is very important to consider when talking about this recovery and stability, that between 1948 and 1952 Germany received - thanks to the Marshall Plan- the sum of 1,400 million dollars.

The bedrock of the Bavarian economy has always been their education. Not because it stands out as a leader in international tests, but because of its technical approach, which consolidated as a valid option within the educational system, matched with a new approach based on industrial exports. The development of the vocational school encouraged technical jobs and future engineers. In *Berufsschule*, young people receive part of their education working in paid internships within companies that usually end up hiring them as permanent employees. This type of education was established as an excellent option that benefits both young people who manage to start a professional career by acquiring early experience in the process, as well as companies that patiently train their future professionals.

The German education system varies considerably from region to region, but it maintains in its base the premise that all children should receive adequate preparation equitably, and for the level of German perfectionism, this means excellence.

About 94% of elementary school students attend a tuition-free government institution. There are private education establishments that are mainly related to the Church. In the PISA 2012 tests, the results of students in public schools adjusted by family purchasing power were better than in private management centres. 87% of adults between 25-34 years of age obtained their secondary degree, above the average of the OECD member countries, which is 82%. As for universities, they are also divided into private and public, with the latter receiving approximately 90-95% of the total enrolment.

Max Weber, one of the most recognized German sociologists, analysed the relationship between capitalism and Protestant ethics, which strongly marked the national idiosyncrasy. Dirk Kaesler, an expert sociologist at Max Weber with an extensive bibliography dedicated to his figure, reflects on the German work culture as follows:

> «Christians, until the Middle Ages and until the beginning of the Modern Age wondered, what will happen to me when I die? Will I go to Heaven or hell? The Catholic solution, originally Christian, was to do good works. We must obey God's commandments, etc. What happens to sinners? Something bad. The Catholic Church has a whole repertoire of rites about forgiveness, confession, etc. The Protestants, on the other hand, focused on the sanctification of work: "Doing good deeds, I will go to heaven." They said: there are usually not that many opportunities for forgiveness. It is

*better to lead this continued lifestyle as a job, as a business so that the result of good works is favourable and abundant. You have to live a life in which every moment, and every situation is dedicated to God. These ideas took root in the Protestant faith. And from there life is run like a business. That brings several consequences: being punctual, being reliable, [...]. My profession is my vocation. What in English is called 'calling'. And increasingly, when people or the world loses their magical element, as Weber said, and people lost faith, there was more independence. The concern was no longer going to heaven but to find a profession that would lead to success. My profession is everything to me »(Oey, Alexander, 2012).*

**Dr. Ulrich Beck, a German sociologist, echoes these words:**

*«You could say that Professor Kaesler's theory summarizes the conflict between northern and southern Europe. Between thrifty Germans and the Catholic South who lead a different, more open lifestyle. [...] "Profession" as a concept of a specific employment situation is a typically German concept. It is almost untranslatable. It is a mixture of class consciousness, quality awareness, competence and ability to focus all that on the market ».*

And he goes on to add:

> «We have a long tradition in the field of education. Humboldtian tradition. Especially in the University (Universität), but also in secondary education (Gymnasium). It is an important foundation of the development of Germany. We differentiate between education (Bildung) and vocational training (Ausbildung). Education is general and vocational training focuses on a trade. In the '70s, I made my first sociological project, an empirical study on the subject. We investigate how to orient the training courses towards the labour market. And the result was very interesting and of wide application: the attempt to achieve useful education is counterproductive, if it's geared nearly solely to jobs. Only a general education makes it possible to adapt because the fast-changing labour market means that after five years after the completion of training these jobs have gone or have almost gone. And those who have received a more general education have greater flexibility to face the changes in the labour market» (Oey, Alexander, 2012).

Germany is currently the sixth largest economy in the world and the most important in the European continent, with a GDP per capita of $ 50,200. It is a world leader in the export of machinery, vehicles, chemicals and benefits from a highly qualified workforce. The 2017 unemployment rate was 3.8% with excellent indicators of income distribution. The fiscal surplus of 2017 was 0.7% with inflation of 1.6%. It chiefly exports high value-added manufactures to the United States, France, the United Kingdom, The Netherlands and China. It mainly imports machinery, technology, vehicles and chemicals from Holland, China, France and Belgium. It is the third producer of alternative energy behind Kenya and Denmark.

The tax system for individual taxpayers is progressive; its tax base is around eight thousand euros by the year and begins by applying a fee of 14% to reach 45% in the top income range (exceeding 270 thousand euros). On the amount paid of taxes, 5.5% of it is calculated, and it becomes an additional "solidarity" tax to cover the continuous costs of integrating the East German states into the country in order to promote their development. There are important deductions on these taxes. Salary deductions for employees on payroll consists of: 7.3% for medical insurance, 1.3% for additional medical insurance, 9.35% for pensions, 1.5% for unemployment insurance and 1.25% for accident insurance, discounting a total of 20.68% of gross salary. All these percentages are matched by the employer, who pays in equal proportions for each of his employees. The above is a very brief summary of a well-known-to-be confusing and complex system. The corporate tax rate is around 30-33% depending on the region.

German tenacity has allowed the country to overcome exceptional challenges with surprising results. Despite the cultural and religious differences of each region, thousands of people marched to the cry of "*Einheit*" (unity) after the fall of the Berlin Wall. The foundation of an inclusive free-market economy where no one is left behind, seeking equality between peers who would now consolidate a single nation, is no accident. The concern is not for the individual good but for the collective good. And the collective good, in the end, is what brings prosperity to everyone. Germany did not follow either the American or the Soviet way, but when reunified it faced its particular destiny making its own way. And on this unknown path that opened in front of them, far from political extremes, much more rational and organized, left the world with a "third way", a new option. It is worth seeing where it leads.

# 5. Singapore

Singapore's miracle: from poverty to wealth in 40 years

Singapore is a small city-state of 5.5 million inhabitants and just 700 km2 with zero natural resources, which has undergone an amazing transformation since its declaration of independence in 1965 - haunted by high indexes of poverty, unemployment and social instability - until present situation as a country exhibiting one of the best standards of living in the world. Because of its particular strategic geographical location, it has become a financial centre that links East and West, favoured by its bilingual education in English and Chinese. From the moment it ceased to be a British colony, the will of the government was to grow through industrialization. To achieve this, the doctrine of "import-substitution industrialization" (ISI) was initially adopted for about fifteen years before rapidly changing it in the late 1970s to the doctrine of "export-oriented industrialization" (EOI), a predominantly liberal model applied in a country with great presence of the State. In a constant search to adapt to the international context, it is currently seeking to transform itself into a "knowledge-based economy" to be globally competitive, with a government willing to change strong paradigms in its population to foster innovation and creativity through education.

Regarding its government, it's far from being a quintessential democracy: a single political party and only three prime ministers have ruled the country from 1965 till today. Very particular circumstances led to its independence, initiating the republic period with high rates of unemployment, housing crisis, poverty and little international confidence about its future. That is why it is considered a miracle that at present the country is at the forefront of the world's standards of living, shining with its own light and being a smart example of proper policy making by reducing poverty gaps, as well as the social disturbances and unrest from its inception. It was the work of Lee Kuan Yew (LKY) that materialized this prodigy, for a period of time that lasted three decades and from its outset raised the flags of social security, free market and zero tolerance to corruption (BBC Mundo, 2015). During the first decade of his term, he solved the problem of the housing deficit by building low-cost state housing and promoting education as an engine for the country's growth. In 1995 LKY handed over the baton of Prime Minister to Goh Chok Tong, who had been his minister since 1981. Years later, Goh decided to step aside and assign the position of Prime Minister to LKY's eldest son and consequently, Lee Hsien Loong has held this position since 2004.

Regarding education, it is predominantly public and of recognized quality, excelling in numerous international tests. At the time of declaring independence, LKY envisioned that in order to develop a local industry and attract foreign investments, It needed a better qualified workforce and implemented an educational system oriented to this purpose in 1968. First, education became bilingual (English as a first language and the possibility of choosing between Chinese, Tamil or Malay as a supplement) to unify multiculturalism and trade more dynamically with the West. Second, education placed special emphasis on mathematics, science and technical subjects. The objective behind these measures was, in the words of the Minister of Education:

> *«[Preserve] equal opportunity for all citizens, established the means of maintaining unity in diversity and instituted a programme for training a new generation for the needs of a forward-looking, modern, industrial and technological society» (Goh Chor Boon, 2006, p. 9)*

It is worth mentioning that this premise is still valid today. The government frequently refers to its population as its only natural resource, and describes education as a "resource development." Primary education was established for all children. The 1960s saw rapid growth in the construction of schools at a rate of a new establishment per month for eight years. The expenditure allocated to this item systematically accounted for 20% of the total public expenditure. At the same time, as the rapid growth of the school population, the number of teachers also expanded in parallel. To meet the needs of a constantly growing student body, large-scale recruitment of teachers was used at the then Teacher Training College. It should also be noted that since 1969 all high-school students received technical education prior to upper secondary school for two years, to encourage the development of both engineers and technical workers. This helped so much that by 1976, 20% of the students in secondary school attended a technical high school. Teachers were also trained in this area in order to keep the teaching force aligned to the objectives of national education.

Towards the end of the '70s, the economic and social indicators illustrated a strong progress in relation to the rest of the emerging countries. It was the result of years of development of the industrial area, mainly forged thanks to the establishment of numerous multinational companies. The manufacturing sector already contributed to 28% of GDP versus 12% in 1960. However, the low-skilled and intensive industrial work that had allowed it to reach this point was no longer a competitive advantage, as the rest of the region began to offer similar possibilities. It was then that a ten-year plan was established with two main strategies: attracting high tech multinational investments and the promotion of activities related to science and technology (for instance: R&D). The education system was revised in 1978 and used as the engine of this new paradigm. This review resulted in a deeply influential document, called "Goh Report," which contained a simple and key observation: during the school stage, children progress at different rates. This brought an issue to surface: if teachers worried about giving a class for the average student, the smartest students would find the school boring and those who had learning difficulties could not keep up with the class. So obvious and so simple, the reaction from the Ministry of Education was decisively to get rid of this inefficiency: the number of years it can take for a primary or secondary school student to complete the cycle, with up to two more years per cycle with a differentiated curriculum (Milne & Mauzy, 1990, pp. 19-20). With the same argument, students who were within 10% of the best performance were detected early to give them a special education. The result was amazing since in just five years, the rate of students who passed the high school completion exam went from 40% to 75% between 1976 and 1985 (Milne & Mauzy, 1990, p. 22). Less than 1% of students dropped out of school without having completed at least 10 years of education.

The improvement of educational quality fuelled an economy growing at a fast pace. By 1995, Singapore led the international science and math tests almost 30% above the rest of the countries (TIMSS 1995 and 1999). The high school was already completed by 96.5% of the students in 1999. Another simple and brilliant idea gave teachers the dynamics necessary to adapt to so many changes: the State began to subsidize 100 hours of training per annum. This had the potential to promote teacher training with an extremely positive effect on the pedagogical system. Additionally, they have an annual stipend of $ 400- $ 700 that they could use in their professional development as they see fit, learning a foreign language, a computer course, buying software, or subscribing to a specialized magazine (Sclafani, Susan, 2008, p. 8). With regard to the salary level, teacher remuneration is even higher than the initial average salary of a lawyer, engineer or doctor at the beginning of the career.

Regarding the health system, it is cheap, of known quality and strongly regulated by the government. The World Health Organization ranked Singapore sixth for its medical system. It is not free; it is complex, and it is divided into three sub-systems:

- Through the "Medisave" program, between 7% and 9.5% of the salary goes to an individual saving (not to a general fund) from which the individual makes the discounts when incurring normal or routine expenses, being able to use these funds both in public hospitals and in private clinics alike. Its scope is such that even drugs are purchased through this personal fund, and it

is the government which determines which drugs enter this list (those that do not enter, have prohibitive prices).
- The following program is similar to the Uruguayan model. It is called "Medishield" and consists of a shelter for costly medical situations. This system is supportive; that is, the savings of all contributors go to a common fund, so premiums are very low. People can choose to exit this program if they wish. It begins to be consumed when the funds available in the "Medisave" program are exhausted or when there is a medical situation out of budget.
- Finally, "Medifund" is government financing for the most vulnerable sector of society, which subsidizes up to 100% of health by analyzing case by case to establish if the user needs it. "Medifund Junior" is a parallel program that deals with the coverage of low-income children, primary care, dental plan, as well as prenatal medicine and obstetrics for the future mother (The Commonwealth Fund, 2017).

The Ministry of Health heavily regulates the sector by granting ratings to private centres and professionals, controlling that advertising is not misleading, publishing a list of medicines that can be purchased through Medisave, and regulating prices. This last point is vital, being the main reason why the expenditure per person in Singapore represents only 30% of the expenditure per person in the USA, providing a clearly higher-quality system to its population (Aaron E. Carroll, 2017). For example, there are public and private hospitals, but public ones are not free but compete equally with private ones.

Another lesson from this fascinating country, is that initially, public and private hospitals were allowed to compete deregulated with the idea that this would lead to the improvement of the national health system by simple market laws. However, this led to hospitals buying new technology at elevated prices, offering high-cost services, paying doctors very differentially and reducing their services to people with fewer resources, focusing on attracting the highest income segment. The consequence was a considerable increase in costs of the health system as a whole, since the higher-income segment paid very high premiums for services that they did not always consume, and it was more expensive for the State to maintain the health system for the more handicapped. When meeting the population needs as a whole, this system was totally inefficient. The price control imposed by LKY made it possible for public hospitals to buy state-of-the-art technology, provide excellent service and pay high salaries to their doctors in a more intelligent and efficient way (Tong, Sheela Narayanan, & Paul, 2015).

Singapore is definitely a very particular case that blends a present and regulatory state with a successful free-market economy. LKY was responsible for providing equal opportunities to the population, and it was the same inhabitants who served as a mean to achieve the deep change that this country went through. When reading its history, it is surprising how the versatility to adapt according to the context without being stuck in a single idea is surprising. When import-substitution industrialization stopped working, the model was changed to an export-oriented industrialization. When the other countries in the region adopted the low-cost labour model, they modified political priorities to generate a context that would attract cutting-edge industries that would generate high added value for the economy and offer outstanding salaries for its inhabitants.

# 6. Denmark

The secret for a public education and healthcare system, full employment, short working hours and economic development

Formed by a peninsula and more than 1,400 islands, its history is closely linked to agriculture. Favoured by its geography, no point in its territory is further than fifty kilometres away from the coast. 80% of the 5.5 million inhabitants speak perfect English. In this flat land where there are more bicycles than cars, live the happiest people in the world -according to the United Nations-, remaining in the top positions of this ranking consistently since the '70s. Perhaps this feature is related to its reduced workday of just 37 hours a week - even less in practice, generally only 34 hours because Fridays work hours in many companies usually end at noon - data that may surprise us when we see Denmark reaching counter-intuitively the third place in terms of productivity among the member countries of the European Union. In fact, strikingly, within the ten countries with the highest GDP among OECD members, seven of them are among those with the least weekly working hours (Denmark, Germany, Luxembourg, Norway, Sweden, Switzerland and The Netherlands). In relation to GDP, it grew 1.3% in 2016 and an approximate rate of 2% is projected for 2017, 2018 and 2019. The unemployment rate fell to what is estimated to be structural unemployment (4.8% in February 2018), so that economy is currently exhibiting excellent indicators. During 2017 Carlsberg, the most important Danish brewery, launched a commercial with the renowned actor Mads Mikkelsen, highlighting the aforementioned virtues of the Danish people. An ingenious invitation to the world to discover a culture in just two minutes, representing the main aspects of national identity.

Its economy had a turning point in the year 1870. This era was marked by the entry of cheaper grains to Europe from the United States of America and the Russian Empire thanks to the improvements in means of transport and the increase in supply. This decrease in international prices directly affected its economy, since it was based primarily on its agricultural sector. Other countries reacted by imposing import tariffs, but Denmark allowed the entry of this economical grain and transformed its productive model by favouring the development of livestock goods of high added value. This transformation happened thanks to the organization of small rural producers grouped in cooperatives that allowed joining forces to seek an associated economic development. The change was successful, and cheap grains were now used to feed its livestock production, allowing advanced techniques to take off by adopting new technologies. The high level of education that population already had at that time was a fundamental factor for the rapid adoption of contemporary ideas and technologies that allowed it to differentiate itself and export products of the highest quality. Danish shortening and bacon continue to be recognized today among the best in the world.

Its industrialization process was postponed till the middle of the 20th century. Even in 1960 the agricultural sector was responsible for most of its exports. At present, it is still a key area, occupying only 6% of the workforce and reaching 40% of total exports. As for industrial activity, it has the surprising record of exporting 80% of its production. A large part of it is high-tech goods manufactured to meet the highest standards. And finally, the participation of the services' sector in its trade balance is growing. To achieve these levels of productivity, Denmark relied throughout its history on a highly qualified and adaptable population.

Education in Denmark is primarily public (Ministry of Higher Education and Science, 2019; OECD, 2014; The Ministry of Higher Education and Science, The Ministry for Children, Education and Gender Equality, & The Ministry of Culture, 2016), with only 13% of students attending private institutions, which must demonstrate that they meet certain standards. Denmark invests 8% of its GDP in education, achieving classrooms with an average of twenty students or less, and a graduation rate greater than 92%. The focus on education is so, that university students receive a grant of up to 900 dollars per month while they study up to a maximum of six years, so that they can complete their career (Ministry of Higher Education and Science, 2019). The main requirement is not to live with their parents in order to receive the total amount. The result is a 48% of population obtaining a tertiary degree. The main target of this system is to avoid socioeconomic background to be a determinant factor to reach their maximum potential, but their skills and interests instead. It works: Danes have one of the highest university graduation rates in OECD member countries and unemployment among young people is 11%, among the lowest in Europe and the United States (Rick Noack, 2015).

Teachers in Denmark lecture fewer hours on average than OECD member countries (650 hours versus 790 hours) and have high salaries. The remuneration for a teacher who has just begun can reach about 45 thousand dollars annually. In order to teach in elementary school, applicants must complete a bachelor's degree in education and a professional practice. High school teachers must have a master's degree in a specific area and complete an annual training. The Ministry of Education campaigns to attract the best students to the teaching area, since it is a career with excellent professional opportunities.

Public health has a long reach and is financed with a 8% tax rate that all workers pay on their gross salary. It covers all expenses of specialists, hospitalization, preventive studies, as well as mental health and long-term care services. Dental services are fully covered for children under 18. Outpatient prescription medications, adult dental care, physiotherapy and optometry services are subsidized. Of the national total, approximately 84% of health expenditures are covered by the State, which represents 10.6% of GDP. An additional system of voluntary coverage provided by non-profit organizations gives 2.2 million people access to supplemental discounts on medications, dental care and physiotherapy. There are many private medical insurances for higher benefits, covering 1.5 million clients (The Commonwealth Fund, 2017). Health spending occupies 30% of total public spending. To evaluate the system, about 250 thousand patients a year are surveyed to know their degree of satisfaction with it. When the doctor prescribes it for very sick or critically ill people, patients are entitled to a nursing service at home with all expenses covered. In addition, the municipalities have comprehensive physical and mental rehabilitation treatments for the patient who cannot take care of himself.

As for those over 65, they have the right to be cared for at home, with professional caregiver, laundry and personal hygiene fully covered. Around 12% of adults over 65 years of age used this type of help in 2017. If the general practitioner detects that the patient needs to go to an asylum to receive more care, the deadline to complete this procedure should not exceed two months. Approximately 4% of adults over 65 are in this type of institutes. Is this an inefficient healthcare system? On the contrary, Danish productivity rates in this area increased steadily (12% from 2007 to 2012), and even having savings, obtained from the elimination of structural inefficiencies. In addition, it is the European country where people spend less time in a hospital (4.5 days on average). This was achieved through a special training focused on general practitioners, who are able to solve about 90% of medical cases in the first consultation, and when there is a patient transferred to a hospital, the high degree of specialization achieved in these institutions allows to treat patients very efficiently in terms of costs. The database of each patient must be shared (even if it was looked after in a private centre), and everyone can check all his information online (Healthcare in Denmark, 2016). In line with the search for the increase in the effectiveness of the system, there is the wonderful possibility of conducting a medical consultation from home through video calling. In the words of Princess Maria Isabel of Denmark:

> *«In Denmark our effort to prioritize the patient - combined with efforts to improve efficiency and quality - resulted in a wide range of innovative solutions in the health sector. I sincerely believe that the achievements and experience achieved*

*can have a positive impact on the health of the whole world»*

In terms of trade, it lines third in the World Bank ranking of "Ease of doing business" behind New Zealand and Singapore, mainly because of its open borders for trade. Its key partners are Germany, Sweden, Norway and England. Its main exports are machinery, chemicals, products of animal origin (pig and fishery) and processed foods. Its core imports are cars, oil, medicines and computers. Denmark stands out for the promotion of the free exchange of goods globally, and argues that all countries, including developing countries, can benefit from an increase in global trade.

Regarding tax, Denmark applies a considerably low rate of 22% for companies' profits (Deloitte, 2018a). All R&D expenses can be deducted from the tax payment. Losses can be transferred to future years without any time restriction. As for taxes on people, the VAT is fixed at 25% for all products. In addition, all taxpayers pay a fixed 8% on gross income that can then be deducted from income tax, when applicable. The income tax is paid from a very low base, is progressive and reaches 55.8% of the total for income greater than $ 500,000 annually. There are several deductions with a limit of 7 thousand dollars per annum to be taken away such as paid interest, child support, and contributions to retirement funds, transportation from home to work and some other concepts (Deloitte, 2018b).

What's the secret of Denmark, in order to be able to provide all these advantages to its population without a significant budget deficit (in the last five years it ranged between a deficit of -1.5% and a surplus of 1% of GDP), with a constant economic growth? Education is the key to success. It always was throughout its history. It was it that allowed Denmark to open its market and go from being a purely agricultural country, to generating livestock products of high added value that achieved worldwide recognition, and still maintain their status. It has a positive trade balance and is an attractive country for foreign investment thanks to its tax system, its capacity for innovation, the country's advanced technology and its excellent professionals. Being a centre for the establishment of companies with high added value, it also obtains benefits in terms of corporate taxes. Not only that, but also the quality of the workforce attracts high-wage industries which increase national exchequer because of the heavy tax burden falling on people. Its health system is likewise vital, allowing the raising of healthy young people, raising awareness in the population about the importance of a healthful life, and taking care of the sickest when they need it most. Such a system allows peace of mind for everyone. And an extremely attractive environment for companies, which have highly qualified human resources and a health system that will keep their employees in good condition. In addition, the control of education and health variables seems to bring a society with better safety rates. Combined with the high productivity of Danish employees, it presents the ideal conditions for a safe investment. The investments compensate greatly for the expense incurred by the government.

# 7. Ireland

The rebel son of the Crown

Land of Celtic legacy, its 800-year struggle with the United Kingdom culminated in its independence in 1922 after which Ireland was proclaimed. Land of an infinite amount of legends and storytelling, the most influential of them is that of St. Patrick, who preached the divine Christian trinity by showing a three-leaf clover ("shamrock"), which would later become a national symbol. Many of these stories reflect the firm character of the Irish people. The most important settlements are located towards the centre and east of the island, where grasslands prevail, in cities such as Dublin, Cork, Limerick or Kilkenny since the west is mountainous, rocky and mostly infertile terrain. The conversion of Ireland to Catholicism was the main reason for confrontation with the British crown throughout its history, and by the beginning of the 20th century, the differences meant the rupture between Ireland and Northern Ireland (which occupies the territory of the former province of Ulster, with an area of approximately one-sixth of the territory of the island), a region of Protestant tradition because of the numerous British settlements that took place there. With the dispute over the northern region increasing after independence, the tension between Catholics and Protestants reached such a point that on Sunday, January 30, 1972 a peaceful civil protest was suppressed by the police, leaving a balance of fourteen dead, in a tragic event that would go down in history as 'Bloody Sunday' (inspiring the famous song of the musical group U2), this being just the beginning of thirty years of attacks executed by the IRA (Irish Republican Army) terrorist organization in an escalation violence known as "The Troubles".

Today it is a very receptive country for those seeking job opportunities in Europe, but ironically its tragic history of pests and wars forced previous generations to massively abandon their lands. The most significant event was the great famine that flogged the territory in the period between 1845 and 1852, where one million people died and more than two million emigrated to Liverpool and the east coast of the United States of America, mainly falling into the cities of Boston, New York and Philadelphia (influence portrayed in different cinematographic works by Martin Scorsese). Of the eight million inhabitants who occupied the territory before this tragedy, the population was reduced by half, and it is today that it barely exceeds five million. Paradoxically, the Irish diaspora resulted in an approximate total of eighty million people around the world possessing Irish roots.

The development achieved by Ireland towards the end of the 20th century qualifies as an economic miracle. During the 1990s, it became the second country with the highest GDP per capita in the Euro zone and the eleventh in the world. This is surprising when comparing the situation in which he was only 30 years ago, in 1987, when The Economist published a famous article entitled "The Poorest of the Rich". The swings suffered by the country throughout the century had several chapters of strong contrasts between them:

- In the 1930s, shortly after becoming independent, Ireland adopted protectionist measures to defend its industry and its farmers. This isolation from the rest of the world extended until the 1950s. The results were economic stagnation, poor development of the national industry and technological backwardness.

- In the 1960s, its policy changed dramatically by adopting free market measures by lowering customs' tariffs and granting tax benefits to companies that invested in their territory. The architect of this opening was Seán Lemass, one of the most respected politicians for his legacy. In parallel, Lemass also established numerous social measures, the most important of which being free primary education.
- In the 1970s, people voted in favour of the referendum to enter the European Economic Community (later, European Union) and continued the implementation of social policies and the expansion of education to include secondary school. Towards the end of this decade, after 20 years of economic opening, the results were not as expected: the welfare state grew bigger than the economy. The budget deficit reached 17% of GDP, remaining only through a level of indebtedness greater than 90% of GDP.
- By the 1980s, the suppression of most trade barriers favoured the elimination of many local producers, rising unemployment to 17% in 1985. Young university students kept emigrating with the consequent loss of skilled labour; tax benefits only attracted small offices mostly dedicated to the final settlement of taxes but not substantial sources of employment; the tax on individual taxpayers reached 60% of income and labour legislation was a disadvantage because of its complexity. Ireland was indeed the poorest country in Western Europe, and the horizon was not encouraging.

- What changed in the 1990s? There were budget cuts, of course, but this measure was not the one that boosted the economy. It is based on the strong commitment of the then Prime Minister Charles Haughey in 1987 aimed at creating a nerve centre for international finance and granting substantial tax benefits (10% income tax for certain financial activities and a cut from 32% to 12.5% for the rest of the companies) which contributed to Ireland starting to create more sources of skilled jobs. The vast majority of multinational companies established their headquarters in Ireland, and their GDP grew between 7.5% and 11.5% for 15 consecutive years.
- As of 2015, according to a report from the Ministry of Finance, the international financial centre employed 35,000 employees in more than 400 firms and was responsible for 7% of GDP. The goal by 2020 is for the sector to occupy a total of 45 thousand professionals (IFS2020: A Strategy for Ireland's International Financial Services sector 2015-2020, 2015).

Education in Ireland is considered a central point in the economic, social and cultural development of Irish society. Governments and the social partners consider it strategically interrelated with national planning. There is a high level of public interest in educational issues, which have been further developed through the consultative approach adopted by the Government in the formulation of educational policy. Irish students excel in international assessments such as the PISA tests, in the subjects of reading and science. Education in Ireland is compulsory from 6 to 16 years of age. The overwhelming majority of schools are funded by the State and the teaching approach is based on each particular case, allowing flexibility in learning times and methods. Despite not being mandatory, virtually all children ages 4 and 5 attend free preschool education. In the 1960s, when education became funded through the State thanks to the government of Seán Lemass, only 20% of students completed secondary education. Slowly, the graduation rate was growing to reach 75% in 1990, laying the groundwork to respond to the demanding challenge in terms of qualified human resources that supposed becoming one of the financial centres of Europe. Currently, more than 80% of students complete high school. At the same time, 43% of the population aged 25-64 have a bachelor's degree, the second highest ratio in Europe only behind the United Kingdom.

Today, it is widely recognized and accepted that education is a key factor of economic success and social progress in modern society. There is growing recognition, particularly in the European Union, that the provision of quality education and training is essential for the creation of an economy based on innovation, and knowledge, which is the basis for continued and sustainable prosperity. Education and training are also crucial to achieve the objective of an inclusive society where all citizens have the opportunity and incentive to participate fully in the social and economic life of the country (Ministry of Education and Science, 2004).

The healthcare system is mixed, with 40% of the population covered by private insurance and the rest depending on public coverage. It has a high private participation in the health system, well above most European countries, and usually has a poor performance in most of its indicators. Waiting lists in the public sector to see a specialist can take up to 18 months. The "European Health Consumer Index" carried out by the Health Consumer Powerhouse is the most comprehensive study on the continent, which gives countries a score between 0 and 1000 points consistently since 2006. The list is headed by The Netherlands with a 924 points score, while Ireland is twenty-fourth among 34 nations with 630 points on the scale. Some points that relegate it are the non-access by law to a second medical opinion, there is no possibility of obtaining shifts online, the very long waiting times, the non-legalization of abortion (in debate at the close of the edition of the book) and inequality between the national and private system. Although the private sector has 40% of the affiliated population, by 2015 public hospitals treated 514,000 patients while private hospitals registered merely 133,000, resulting in a clear imbalance between resources and expenses of each. The Irish government invests only 5.5% of its GDP, far from 8.5-9% occupied by countries that lead the health rankings such as Norway, Sweden and Denmark.

The standard of living is high in Ireland; wages rose from the time of the Celtic Tiger to the present, and inequality decreased due to its redistributing tax system. The population has a good balance between personal life and work, feels safe and has strong social ties. Tax cuts boosted the revival of global post-crisis financial consumption (2008-2009), and the unemployment rate for 2017 was 6.4%. The economy projects a continuous growth of the order of 2-3%, and the inflation rate will not exceed 2%. The biggest threat that falls on its economy is how Brexit will impact its exports since the UK absorbs 20%

of them. The health system generates discontent in the population, but reforms are projected to make it more efficient to reduce waiting times and to give free access to the general practitioner for the entire population. Ireland transformed its country model with surprising results. He learned in the toughest way that isolated policies fail and a comprehensive solution with solid foundations on which to build a model is necessary.

## 8. Canada

The world embassy of diversity

It is the second largest country on the planet and houses an estimated two million lakes in its territory. The history of Canada is a history of integration and tolerance: a pioneer in terms of individual freedoms, it was the American slaves who first sought refuge in their territory since slavery began to be illegal from several particular judicial decisions since the decade of 1790 in the provinces of Quebec and Ontario. Then, with the construction of the coast-to-coast railway, Asian immigration grew considerably, a feature that can be observed today in its demographic composition. The current population is approximately 35 million inhabitants, which are identified with more than 250 different ethnic groups (40% of the total is identified with more than one origin at a time). At the 2016 census, the most represented groups were English, Scottish, French, Irish, German, Chinese, Indian, Italian, Aboriginal, Ukrainian, Dutch, Polish, Filipino and Russian («North America: Canada — The World Factbook — Central Intelligence Agency », 2019).

Its economic growth is undoubtedly linked to that of the United States, the only country with which it shares almost nine thousand kilometres of border to the south and west of its territory - the most extensive border between any two countries in the world. Its vast extension was blessed with abundant natural resources that position it as the economy with the third-largest oil reserve behind Venezuela and Saudi Arabia and the sixth largest producer of crude oil. Its degree of economic integration with the United States is such that three-quarters of its exports are destined for its neighbouring country. Its export matriz is composed as follows:

- 24% minerals and metals
  - Crude oil (9%) and refined oil (2%)
  - Iron
  - Copper
  - Coal
  - Aluminum
  - Nickel
- 19% transport
  - Cars and vehicle parts
  - Aircrafts and components
- 7% chemical products
  - Medicaments
  - Fertilizers
  - Radioactive chemicals
- 5% mineral products
  - Gold

Its imports have the following composition:
- 26% machines
  - Computers
  - Broadcasting equipment
- 17% transport
  - Cars and vehicle parts
  - Aircraft parts
- 8% mineral products

In summary, it is a highly diversified economy, where natural resources represent 50% of total exports and is the main source of income for several provinces. At the same time, it has a broad industrial structure, concentrated in the main urban centres. It is highly dependent on trade, forming part of the NAFTA free trade agreement and having separate treaties with a large number of countries, including Chile, Costa Rica, Israel, Peru, Iceland, Switzerland and Norway. There are no extensive government controls on the prices of goods and services in Canada, except for some monopolistic services that are under review by specific committees (Deloitte, 2017).

Regarding education in Canada, it is mostly public, where 94% of the tuition is concentrated. 91% of adults between 25-64 years of age completed secondary education and 57% of them obtained a bachelor's degree. The government invests approximately 5% of GDP in education. What's the secret of this excelling outcome without excessive spending? According to Andreas Schleicher, Director of Education of the OECD, "the theme that unites is equity" because despite the different approaches to education in each province, there is a common commitment to equal opportunities in school. He also mentions that there is a great sense of justice and equal access, which is reflected in the high academic performance of the children of immigrants, who from the third year since their arrival obtain a slmllar score in international exams as their peers, something extraordinary if we consider the rest of the member countries of the organization. In addition, he mentions that a primary factor is the high-level salary paid to the teachers, who have to overcome an arduous process in order to lecture in front of students. There is a strong awareness of help, so when a school is identified or a student is in difficulty, the cause is immediately sought to empower both the establishment and the students. The schools, therefore, have an exceptionally homogeneous performance. As a result, in the most recent PISA exams the variation in the score caused by socio-economic differences was only 9%, very little in relation to 20% in France or 17% in Singapore (Islam, 2017).

The Canadian public health system is known to many, but not the transformation it went through since until the mid-twentieth century, it was a private system similar to that of the USA (The Commonwealth Fund, 2017). In 1910, a very humble child almost lost his leg due to an infection because his parents could not cover the cost of treatment. In 1944, this boy named Tommy Douglas won the governorship of the province of Saskatchewan in the centre of the country and established a universal coverage system that would become the model adopted at the federal level in the short span of ten years, to become a pillar fundamental worthy of national pride, with an approval greater than 90% of the population (Amanda Coletta, 2018).

In the words of Tommy Douglas :

> «I felt that no child should have to depend - either on his leg or on his life - on his parents' ability to raise enough money to bring a first class surgeon to his side of the bed»(Shackleton, 1975, p. 17)

The provinces began to subsidize the population's expenses in private institutions by reimbursing the total medical expenses in hospitals or clinics and covering emergency expenses. At present, the health system is financed through general taxes with a significant distortion in spending between the different provinces due to demographic factors such as very small or dispersed populations in the interior provinces. When a Canadian requires medical attention, the first contact (mandatory) is with the general practitioner who may be located in hospitals, local centres or private offices, and they are themselves responsible for requesting reimbursement to the government for the service they provided, removing patients of this responsibility. If necessary, the generalist refers you to a hospital or an appropriate professional. Pubic coverage generally only includes dental plan, ophthalmology, prostheses, wheelchairs and physiotherapy for adults, children and low-income people. The rest of the citizens has to pay these expenses out of pocket or take out private insurance (approximately 66% of the population has this type of insurance, which is financed in 94% of the cases by employers as a benefit to their wage earners) but are prohibited by law from providing a service that the State takes over. Canada spends less than the United States per citizen and has better indicators on life expectancy, obesity, infant mortality and mortality from treatable diseases.

The main criticisms to the system are the long waiting times (43% received medical attention on the same day; 50% had delays longer than two hours in emergency rooms; 30% waited more than two months to see a specialist; 18% suffered delays greater than four months for certain surgeries according to data from the Commonwealth Fund); and Canada carries the burden of being the only developed country with universal health that does not cover medications. In addition, numerous medical articles speak of an outdated system, since it did not undergo major changes in the last fifty years while the needs of the population mutated due to the general demographic aging. At present, the centralized hospital model is not efficient for the treatment of chronic diseases such as diabetes, dementia, cardiology and chronic lung diseases whose patients would not need to be hospitalized.

The tax rate on individual taxpayer varies considerably from province to province. It can reach from 20% to 58.75% in the province of Quebec, where the highest rate can be found. As for the corporate tax rate, it consists of a fixed 15% nationwide, plus a provincial rate that can vary between 11% and 16% (Deloitte, 2017).

Canada obtains high rates of general well-being, employment and income, health, education, social life and personal safety, components of the OECD Measured Welfare Index. The levels of income and wealth of households are above the OECD average, while the results in employment, income and access to housing are well above the OECD average. It does not perform so well in relation to the balance between personal life and work.

Canada is a country full of opportunities, where a large number of immigrants seek to improve their personal situation. One in five inhabitants of Canada was born abroad, and OECD studies show an integration into the country that exceeds that achieved in the rest of the member countries. The chances of obtaining a good education are superior to the rest and their results in international exams show an exceptionally satisfactory adaptation. Statistically, here immigrants have no problem in achieving a welfare similar to the locals. As for the population in general, citizen participation in politics is high, with 68% of the population taking part in the general elections. Regarding the government, only 36% of Canadians indicated that they believe corruption is common, a figure far below the 56% obtained by the countries that make up the OECD (OECD, 2017a).

Home of stunning landscapes, Canada is rarely a reference country to visit, but it can easily attract the attention of tourists in search of spectacular panoramas and adventure. In fact, the most important pictorial movement in its history, "the group of 7", was a group of artists who portrayed countless landscapes around the country. One of the main collections can be found in the Art Gallery of Ontario, in the city of Toronto. The Canadian citizen is generally a person who is constantly searching for a balance between a government that offers equal opportunities, adequate health services and quality education, while recognizing the importance of attracting foreign investments to improve their economy. A country that does not aspire to be exemplary, with humble people and rulers, but that ironically leaves valuable lessons to the rest of the world.

# 9. South Korea

"Miracle on the Han River"

Isolated from the mainland because of the violent war that developed on the Korean peninsula between 1950 and 1953, the contrast between communist North Korea and capitalist South Korea could not be greater. The military confrontation left a balance of 1.5 million civilian casualties and more than half of the country's infrastructure destroyed. The conflict was unfinished as peace had never been signed, and consequently, a demilitarized border four kilometres wide are maintained, until now, heavily guarded by both countries in a tense calm. The quality of life achieved by South Korea after its economic miracle known as "The Miracle of the Han River" (in reference to the "miracle of the Rhine River" that underwent West Germany after World War II) allowed its population to reach In recent decades, a quality of life was unthinkable after the independence of Japan in 1945, when it was in social and political chaos.

After a span of three years of American occupation over the territorial dispute between the USA, China and the USSR, it had its initial democratic government in 1948, when Korea went down a road that alternated violent military and civil governments that only shared their high corruption rates. Towards the beginning of the '60s, this peninsula with very few natural resources, agricultural economy and extended poverty, with a budget that depended on 50% of foreign aid, suffered its first coup d'état. Park Chun Hee led the uprising that led him to govern the nation from 1961 to 1979, focusing his efforts on creating an export-linked economy (similar to Singapore) and granting for this purpose extraordinary benefits to the most important families of the country. This gave rise to the traditional South Korean "Chaebols": extraordinarily diversified large conglomerates whose translation is at the same time "family business" and "monopoly", which laid the foundations for companies such as Samsung, Daewoo, Kia, LG or Hyundai. These business conglomerates diversified to the point that they became the largest labour demand in the country. Time would make Park Chun Hee right, as these policies favouring free markets did not disrupt the national industry, and the export orientation allowed GDP growth with extraordinary rates for more than 30 years. In 2004, Korea joined the select group of countries with a GDP that exceeds one billion dollars. All this, regardless a Japanese report issued by their government in 1961 than claimed «*The Korean economy has a dark future to establish economic growth and self-sufficiency due to its overpopulation, resource shortages, underdeveloped industry, high military cost, political disability, weak national capital and administrative disabilities*».

The economic success underwent in the second half of the twentieth century shared similar characteristics along with Hong Kong, Singapore and Taiwan, nations that the world would call Asian Tigers for its booming economy and its huge industrialization rates (World Bank, 1993). Today, South Korea is the seventh largest exporting economy in the world, the largest producer of ships and the first exporter of chips and memory cards. It has free trade agreements with more than fifty countries and in recent years its economy grew at an approximate rate of 3%. Its unemployment rate is 3.4% and has very positive income distribution rates, with the poorest 10% obtaining around 6.8% of total income while the richest 10% records 48.5% of it. The Gini coefficient, which measures this disparity, yields an index of 34.1 for the country. An intermediate result between the 21.5 disparity in Finland and the 42.7 in Argentina. The middle class is made up of a high percentage of the employees of the chaebols to which all local workers aspire. Those who manage to enter these companies enjoy a high status in society and usually aspire to live in the richest neighbourhood of the city of Seoul, Gangnam District. This neighbourhood concentrates fashion, cafes, culture, music, the best restaurants and the most coveted homes, which can reach values of 10 thousand dollars per square meter. The K-pop movement (Korean pop) dominates the music scene and crossed the borders with singer PSY through the most watched video in YouTube history, Gangnam Style, which means that when a person has a certain style and status they can afford to live in this wealthy district. It is no coincidence then that Korea has a high debt rate among its population, which finances these high costs of living with a growing financial debt.

During the 1960s, even though it was an extremely poor nation, it concentrated its efforts in the textile industry, becoming the world's leading exporter. However, this low-wage-based model soon ceased to be competitive and the government sought to develop more productive sectors such as steel, ship and machinery construction. The impulse of the steel industry allowed the country to provide raw material for the improvement of the naval industry, cars, advanced machinery, construction and electronics. To encourage the development on stage, they hired Japanese specialists to import the knowledge that would allow them to improve their ability to produce technology, and when technological limitations arose, they were solved with great creativity, allowing Korean industry to advance to the forefront of global technological development. During the 1970s, it used the two oil crises that followed to expand its borders and deploy its enterprises in the oil industry in the Middle East. The '80s saw the arrival of large foreign investments, with the Asian Tigers already consolidated as attractive economies for world capitals (Barro, 1998). This flow of investments produced a financial bubble in the 1990s that exploded in 1997, and South Korea went bankrupt. The IMF went to the rescue to finance the deficit but imposed its conditions. These forced to close insolvent financial institutions, restructure local holdings, encourage cultural changes in the chaebols to encourage competition and increase employee performance. By August 2001, Korea cancelled its debt with the IMF and its level of reserves reached approximately 100 billion dollars.

The university is the gateway to a better life and drastically determines the future jobs a person can obtain. Rumour has it among students, that the most important companies in the country hire only those who acceded one of the top three universities in the country, discarding the profiles of those who attend other institutions, without stopping in any other detail. 70% of the population has a university degree, the highest percentage of OECD member countries. Education is culturally vital for families without correlation with another society in the world. The importance of education in order to become the economic power that it is today is deeply rooted in people, and that translates into families who sacrifice everything to provide the best possible opportunities for their children. 97% of young people between 25-34 years old completed their secondary education, the highest percentage registered among OECD member countries. South Korea always ranks first in the PISA international exam rankings. The main explanation is that the Park government understood that to develop the industry it required skilled labour, so the government aligned the curriculum with its strategic needs, which translated into an approach geared towards the exact sciences and mathematics, subjects in which they exceed the rest of the OECD countries.

The education system is so relevant that the qualifying degree for teaching in Korea grants great prestige, and is achieved only after going through an extremely rigorous career that is rewarded with high salaries. In order to be able to access the teaching career, it is necessary to have obtained qualifications within 5% higher at the end of compulsory education. In order to match the level of all educational establishments, both teachers and principals and assistant directors rotate through a raffle system every four or five years from one school to another within the district where they live. The same lottery system is used for student entry, in order to avoid educational segregation. The elementary school and middle school are mandatory and fully covered by the government, while the high school and the popular extracurricular classes are taught in private institutions and represent a significant outlay for parents. The elementary school runs from 8 am to 9.30 pm or even until 11 pm in the overcrowded Hawgons: massive private extracurricular school support classes that move a $ 200 million business. Through the Hawgons, young people intend to increase their chances of performing well the annual entrance exam to universities, which determines the range of options to choose through the qualification obtained. The exam arrives unfailingly on the second Thursday of each November, and the country stops for 600,000 students to decide their fate during the eight hours that the exam lasts. It literally stops, as flights are rescheduled and buildings that take place near the venues where exams are taken are cancelled in order to avoid any confusion among students. Only by obtaining 490 of the 500 possible points, students can access one of the three top universities that will open the doors to a promising future (Wizenberg & Varsavsky, 2017). In the elite Hawgons there are employees who walk among the students waking them up if they fall asleep after several days of study. Throughout the school year, it is very strange to find a child that repeats the year.

    This level of stress in adolescents is priced too high: suicide rates in South Korea are the highest in the world, especially between the ages of 10 to 19, a period in which the government recently found that at least 50% of young people thought of suicide as a means of escape from the pressure imposed both socially and by the family environment. The support provided by the State for this problem is still insufficient and inefficient. As a counterpart to this problem, incipient non-traditional schools emerged to contain children looking for another type of training. They encourage discussion, critical capacity and creativity, an approach that lies at the antipodes of the standard and mathematical orientation of the traditional school, with a much smaller time load. In conclusion, despite being extremely inefficient - to the point of costing the lives of young people - the educational system fulfils its purpose: it creates a technical differentiation in its population to attract work and investments, with a highly qualified workforce.

Korea offers antagonistic strategies, with transcendental sectors jealously guarded through limitations on the entry of foreign capital (both in industry and in Internet services and in cultural and television content) combined with attractive tax benefits for the rest of economic activities. As an example, it offers a five-year tax exemption for the installation of high-tech companies, which increases the demand for skilled labour and attracts high value-added investments that also provide knowledge to society. With regard to corporate tax, it has a complex and progressive system according to the level of earnings that can be summarized as follows:

- Big enterprises:
    - Income tax: progressive from 10% untill 22%
    - Retained income tax: 10% of retained income tax, with a deduction on disbursements regarding investments, salary raises and dividend payments.
- SMEs:
    - Income tax: fixed rate of 7% with special benefits that allow discounts until 4% is reached.
- Individual taxpayer:
    - Progressive from 6% up to 44% with a great range of possible deductions.
- Losses:
    - Carryforward: 10 years

Korea is currently facing an incipient growth in relation to social inequality (OECD, 2016), pollution and corruption, but having emerged from a context of war and extreme poverty, the results obtained in the last 50 years are encouraging. Its transformation reached a spectacular metamorphosis, going from a country whose budget depended upon 50% from foreign aid, in a critical situation, to provide assistance to Eastern Europe, Asia, Africa, the Middle East and Central America. The way out of poverty was not easy, and all its inhabitants know that it was education and hard work that allowed them to realize this economic miracle in a country without natural resources, so these values are deeply rooted in their culture.

# 10. Finland

The country with the best educational system in the OECD

Exhibit the best education system throughout the world is a sufficient introduction for the easternmost territory of the Nordic countries, whose location halfway between Russia and Sweden was strategic for both empires. From the twelfth to the eighteenth century, it was part of the kingdom of Sweden and from 1809 until his independence in 1917, he was part of the Russian Empire. With approximately 80% of its land covered by woodlands, it transformed its economy, from an agricultural and forestry economy to a modern diversified and technological infrastructure. Interestingly, it is the only Nordic country that is a full member part of the European Union since 1999.

Finland has a high industrial development, and is characterized by an extensive free-market economy with a GDP per capita in the order of Austria and The Netherlands, and slightly higher than in Germany and Belgium. Trade is central, with exports representing more than a third of GDP and a government constantly looking for external investments. It is historically competitive in manufacturing, particularly in the forestry, metallurgical, engineering, telecommunications and electronics industries. This is so, because being the country in the region farthest from the equator, its lands present a great challenge for the development of agriculture. It stands out in the export of technology and is the cradle of numerous high-tech and computer enterprises, games, renewable energy and biotechnology. Forestry, an important export industry, provides a secondary occupation for the rural population ("Europe: Finland — The World Factbook — Central Intelligence Agency", 2019).

Finland achieved sustained development up to the 2009 worldwide housing crisis, but got around it avoiding extreme consequences. However, the global slowdown drastically affected exports and domestic demand, which caused a contraction of the economy in the period from 2012 to 2014. The recession hit a government that incurred large public spending to provide a welfare state to its population, seeking financing in the international market. The economy grew again from 2016, registering an increase of 1.4% of GDP and a 3.3% projected for 2017, backed by a sharp increase in investment, private consumption and net exports. GDP is expected to grow 2-3% in the coming years. With 5.5 million inhabitants and an economically active population of 2.7 million people, the crisis left a high unemployment rate of around 8.1%.

During the post-World War II period, the country was far behind the rest of the industrialized countries in terms of development and GDP per capita. It was then that Finland favoured an export-oriented economy, developing in the first phase the pulp mills for papermaking (taking advantage of its extensive forest resources) and light metallurgical. Tax incentives were offered to external investments, and a profound change was initiated in the education system that would lay the foundation for a knowledge-based society and cutting-edge technology. From this impulse to education, the focus was to give importance to both mathematics and science, as well as to the development of critical and creative capacity. Towards the end of the 1980s, Finland already had a per capita income among the highest in developed countries. Russia was always a key trading partner for the country, and when its neighbour collapsed in the early 1990s, the Finnish economy was hit hard, but not dejected. In the years after the fall of the Berlin Wall, the macroeconomic situation stabilized and the economy revitalized. The government incentive towards telecommunications allowed the emergence of the giant Nokia. Among his contributions to the world is the development of the Angry Birds game and the Linux operating system.

The education system did not stand out until the 1970s over others around the world. They had low rates of graduation, participation, efficiency and equality. In the post-war era, the main objective of the educational authorities became the creation of a system that could provide equal opportunities, which would guarantee the country a suitable population to face the challenge represented by new technologies, promote democratic values and could allow each individual to reach their full potential. From these premises, a stage of transformation began in schooling. The old elementary school of rigid structures resulted in a new, more flexible system that delayed the choice of career guidance until the last few years. The teaching method became more personalized and the requirements for teachers to be able to teach became more demanding. The entire educational structure is funded by the government, including university higher education, which is also free for foreigners –if someone dares to learn Finnish-.

To enter the teaching school, it is necessary to have obtained grades within the top 10% in high school. Religion is part of the national identity, with the vast majority of the Lutheran population. This is important when talking about education because in the past, in order to get married and have children, it was necessary to prove before the Church that the couple could read and write, which generated a culture that gave learning a preponderant role. Children do not start schooling after the age of 7 (one year later than the rest of their European peers), with a preschool year between 6 and 7. Nevertheless, in reality, the children attend as early as three years to centres that focus on social development. Students attend school until the age of 16, when they go to high school extending the same for three years choosing between general or vocational training. Everything is paid by the government, including transportation and study material. Education in Finland is considered a human right.

The model adopted in the seventies has some remarkable points:
- Excellence through equal opportunities is a priority for both educators and policy makers. Finnish schools have the smallest differences from each other, compared to the rest of the OECD member countries (PISA 2012). No father in Finland cares about finding the best school, because they are all very similar to each other.
- Finnish teachers are responsible for informing each student's progress to parents, as there are no standardized tests to measure them. By having a low number of students per class, each teacher knows perfectly the degree of progress of each of their students and can help them to progress in a personalized way when they have difficulties.
- Teachers assign a low homework load to children between the ages of 11 and 14, usually half an hour per day. In home school between 7 and 11 years, homework assignments are particularly unusual.

- Finland got rid of standardized tests based on the principle that each child is different, progresses at different rates and has their own interests.
- The cost per student is highly efficient: it surpassed by more than 60 points the United States, Norway and Austria in the PISA exams with a cost 45% lower in terms of percentage of GDP.
- Year after year they select the best graduates to access to study the primary school teacher career. It is one of the most competitive careers. Of the 5,000 to 7,000 postulates, only between 650 and 700 are accepted. Candidates are required to possess artistic (dance, sing, paint, be a musician) or sports qualities, in addition to having excellent qualifications in science and mathematics. It is very strange that a teacher abandons teaching, which greatly decreases the cost of the education system.

Pasi Sahlberg, a global prophet of the virtues of the system, dramatically distinguishes the Finnish educational system from the one that predominates in the most accepted reforms from the 1990s to the present. He calls them "Global Educational Reform Movement", or GERM for its acronym (this is intentional, since he describes them as a virus that is spread and causes a disease in the educational system):

- Under "global reform", there is a focus on academic subjects in the first years of primary school such as mathematics, while the Finnish model seeks a more comprehensive education to give stronger tools to its students (social sciences, art and music). Sahlberg

argues that the objective is to maintain a balance between academic subjects and the development of creativity.
- Under "global reform", a standardization of education is sought to impart the same content to all children. Sahlberg argues that the best approach is one that focuses on the student in a personalized way to help him progress at his own pace and with the topics that arouse most interest. In high school this is accentuated, since each student follows their own curriculum.
- Under "global reform", competition among students is encouraged, which results in a high degree of stress for young people. By definition, the competition will leave many children aside. Sahlberg argues that while competition is culturally encouraged in Finland, this is not the case for education, where the goal is to enrich all students so that everyone can develop their greatest potential.
- Under the "global reform", a greater variety of schools is encouraged so that there is a greater possibility of choice, generating differences between one establishment and another. In Finland, all establishments are very similar to each other and no parents worry about choosing a school for their children. The degree of personalization of education during your school life gives you this possibility and further improves the chances of choosing your own path for each student.

Newsweek immortalized in its cover of August 2017 the election of Finland as the best country in the world to live. The premise from which the magazine started was: "If you were born today, which country would provide you with the best opportunity to live a healthy, safe, reasonably prosperous life and possibilities of social ascent?" Finland also has one of the lowest rates of perceived corruption in the world, ranking third behind Denmark and New Zealand.

# What to do next

*Conclusion:*

What makes a successful nation? In conclusion, we can find certain points in common that are worth highlighting.

*Free markets:*

Undoubtedly, the elimination of trade barriers is a central point that all analysed countries share. The greater the economic integration with the world, the greater commercial exchanges will grow, allowing free trade to provide jobs and an incremental GDP. However, this is risky, since the greatest lesson after Ireland's analysis is that opening up to the global market must be done in a strategic and orderly manner to be successful. And this is obvious, if we think that a country cannot be integrated to the world if it has nothing to offer. Two key points are repeated unfailingly through the analysis: a protection of the State to key sectors of its economy and a differential factor that attracts investments offering the world a distinctive added value. Norway protects its commercial airspace; Switzerland protects its farmers not only because of its inability to compete with international prices but also because they occupy a fundamental role in the care of the rural area. Korea protects its chaebols, its financial services and telecommunications. This protection is generally not based on the profitability of the mentioned sectors but on strategic reasons of national interest. Regarding the differential factor, we find that skilled labour is a characteristic that crosses a wide range of cultures and economies to become the most relevant shared theme. Natural resources are undoubtedly a base on which to rely on the development of an economy, but Switzerland, Singapore, Ireland, South Korea and Finland have very few natural resources without this having prevented them from spectacularly growing their GDP. Switzerland offers its financial services with highly skilled labour and tax advantages; Singapore differs through its highly skilled workforce and its export orientation; Ireland with its financial services centres with differential tax benefits; South Korea with its highly qualified workforce (70% of the population has a bachelor's degree) and its export orientation. All of them benefit from global trade because they provide a product with high added value that makes their GDP grow, and they benefit from the best offers in the international market when importing.

At the same time, it is vital to note the threat that constitutes an insertion to the global market devoid of a solid strategy, since there is a latent threat to the internal economy. The aforementioned case of the Ireland of the '60s, opening its borders to world trade after years of isolation had very negative results, such as its high-poverty rates, destruction of local production, massive emigration of young people in working-age and the resulting economic crisis. In Argentina, we suffered exactly the same consequences of increased poverty and unemployment, destruction of regional economies and crisis when eliminating trade barriers during the last decade of the previous century.

*Education:*

Throughout the Argentine territory, roughly 30% of young people attend private education institutions, with a graduation rate of 66% nationwide. The proportion is inverse in public managed institutions were approximately 70% of students attend with a graduation rate of 33%, according to a report from the Centre for Education Studies Argentina of the University of Belgrano (September 2017).

At the same time, the 2010 national census showed that 61% of people over 20 years old had not completed their secondary education.

Unlike the vast majority of countries we've been evaluating, in the Latin-American continent, enrolment in private institutions increased these recent years: Argentina, Uruguay, Chile, Brazil, Peru, Colombia and Mexico saw a growth of students in private institutions from a 15% in the year 2000 to 18% in the year 2010. Each case deserves a detailed analysis, but there is a manifest segregation between upper-class families, and those families which do not have the resources to invest in their children instruction (if they do invest, the proportion of their income spent is significantly greater) (Rivas, 2015).

In the PISA tests of 2012, 63% of Latin American students scored below the expected minimum in mathematics, 49.6% in science and 46% in reading. The students here get worse grades than Western Europe, Eastern Europe, Anglo-Saxon countries, Asia Pacific and Nordic countries, and at the same time these scores are well below the OECD average.

It is easy to see that education in successful countries is mostly public and free, thus providing equal opportunities to all children, but it is necessary to stop and analyze several issues. First, a private education system is by definition a sewer of differences. Imagine for a moment that 100% of education is now privately managed. What would happen in such a model? According to INDEC (National Statistics Agency in Argentina) data, the poorest 10% in Argentina have an income in the second quarter of 2017 of approximately AR$ 1,600*, 15% below indigence. The most vulnerable population does not have the necessary means to meet the cost of quality education.

If the goal pursued with private managed schools is to compete for some private entrepreneurs to offer a better education than the rest, it means mathematically that at the opposite end, there will be other institutions with poor results that will not achieve the national targets, precisely because of the encouraged competition. It is clearly exclusive, since only a handful of students will be able to access institutions with the best resources at their disposal and superior results. And in this market experiment, the *ex post* victims are those children who received a deficit education that the system itself encourages.

In every economy, there are lower quality by-products that meet the same need, but are aimed at different customers with different purchasing power. Therefore, if education remains in the hands of private entrepreneurs, there will always be projects that do not focus on quality but on price. If

---

* USD 98 at a 16.32$/USD Exchange rate
  USD 137,80 at a 'purchase power parity' of 11.61 (IMF, Implied PPP conversion rate)

we let this happen in the educational field, the by-product of lower quality will be the pedagogy of a child, which unfortunately will not develop its full potential in the economy, resulting in a nations' disadvantage. Popular knowledge teaches us that in the long term, "As you sow, so shall you reap". And if we sow inequality in pursuit of finding the best results for some through the market rules, the harvests on the other side of the scale are the children, victims of the institutions registering deficient results.

The next question is whether it is okay for children to be inescapably linked to economic possibilities and parents' decisions. Some people may argue that if the family has the financial opportunities to pay for the best possible education, he should be able to do so, while the education of the most disadvantaged may not be the best but this is a consequence of his parents' decisions.

But if the most disadvantaged population does not have access to quality education, it is not just poor disadvantaged people who suffer the consequences, but the whole country. For instance, in Argentina, without full secondary education it is statistically more difficult to enter the labour market, and the 2010 census indicated that 61% of Argentines over 20 years old did not complete their studies. This is a regional disadvantage that hits the whole nation. Without qualified work you cannot attract or generate investments with high added value. Consequently, the absence of this qualified workforce leaves the country out of global competition, harming the population as a whole. In addition, an increase in unemployment creates conditions conducive to a consequent increase in insecurity. Wouldn't we rather live in a safe society, perhaps? Wouldn't we rather live in a country that is a powerhouse, which has a high GDP per capita and where high value-added investments are generated? A society of these characteristics would benefit the people as a whole.

On the other hand, providing equal opportunities for all children is not just a progressive, benefactor and solidarity discourse. Equal opportunities is a strategic issue that allows a country to offer a labour market at its greatest potential, it is the ability of a country to reach 100% of its capability and to differentiate itself, with the consequent appeal to any investor. The opposite of this is inefficiency, it is the inability of a nation to develop each and every one of its inhabitants to be their own best version. And it is not a minor detail, because from the point of view of the investor when choosing the destination of his capital between one country or another, it is preferable to do it where not only 30% of people reached a high degree of professionalism but where 100% of people can offer great results. It is without any doubt a better investment that will generate a greater added value to the company, which will produce a differential.

It is worth mentioning that countries with public education systems are also the most efficient in terms of expenditure, measured as a percentage of GDP. Argentina invests - in the sum of public spending and private effort - 7.1% of its Gross Domestic Product in education with discouraging results. Regarding this point, the search for budget efficiency is a central issue to the OECD, and has become a priority in recent decades, being Finland one of the nations that manages to stand out from the rest and obtain results well above the average, justifying at least a more in-depth analysis. A possible explanation for this efficiency may be that the resources invested in privately managed institutions take away resources from the traditional public school. In addition, the expense that parents pay monthly for the education of their children is necessarily the source of miscellaneous expenses (advertising, high salaries of school owners). In addition, by not sharing resources among the different private institutions, and competing with each other, they spend their funds inefficiently.

Which policies can be put into practice in Argentina? It is necessary to enhance the quality of national education so that it can compete in quality with private management teaching institutes. It is vital to emphasize that the recovery of the public system must be through free competition in a market where each parent can choose the educational establishment. In order to achieve these objective, several problems must be addressed:

- School days: one of the main concerns, for which throughout Latin America there is a migration from public to private schools, are the several teacher strikes. Educators claim for their rights but governments in general do not give in, even on long periods of inactivity. These strikes trigger the perfect combo for the system's decline: teachers generally have sufficient reasons to complain, the government knows it but is not interested in negotiating, and families choose to migrate to private institutions, guaranteeing their children's education. A process of privatization, conscious or unconscious, but that is happening right now throughout the whole continent.

- Teachers: two problems stand out:
    - Salaries: annual teaching salaries in dollars in public institutions increased from USD 12,377 in 1998 to USD 17,041 in 2010, an improvement of 38% in nominal terms (in line with the regional average increase). Data from 2010 places Argentina below Chile, where they earn roughly USD 23,500 (a notable improvement of 123% compared to the 10,500 in 1998 that validates the results of the educational riots that took place in the neighboring country). Despite this, when comparing the local figures with the OECD member countries, salaries are approximately 50% lower than the average, while the regular salary is 30% below the average.
    - Professional quality: Times change rapidly, and a speedy adaptation of the teaching staff is necessary to carry out their work without losing quality. The solution to this problem in Singapore was to subsidize 100 hours of training freely chosen by the teacher. This is a key tool that enhances the abilities of those interested in regularly improving their skills.
- Classroom size: a smaller classroom allows a high-quality follow up, strengthening the development of each student. There is a growing investment in numerous countries that aim at better educational quality to provide classes with less than 20 students.
- Individual and digital education: a most personalized dedication allows each student to learn at their own

pace and on the topics that interest them most. If teachers face a very large course and are forced to lecture all children with the same concepts, there is a setback: each child learns at a different pace, and we must accept this reality without prejudice. If teachers focus on the average student, children who have slower learning capabilities will not be able to keep up, and the more advanced ones will get bored. If teachers can give them differentiated attention, they would focus on a more flexible teaching plan. Allowing everyone to assimilate basic concepts in a most appropriate way.

*Healthcare:*

Counter-intuitively, the countries with the highest participation of private companies providing health services are those with the most expensive medicine in terms of GDP percentage. The United States and Switzerland are clear examples. Free competition does not immediately translate to savings. Singapore has a very interesting answer that is worth noticing. At some point in their history, they allowed a deregulated system of private medical insurance but found it inefficient (Aaron E. Carroll, 2017). The richest paid a "price premium" in relation to the use they made of the service, while public health services did not provide enough quality for disadvantaged patients. Dumping idle resources favouring one sector of society in detriment of another in a service that necessarily covers 100% of the population, is a costly structural deficiency. The system that Singapore established, it is worth remembering, is that personal or family group medical expenses are taken from an individual fund, raised through a monthly deduction from salaries.

***Final notes:***

A healthy, educated and productive population has the ability to become an asset and reduce unemployment. This results in the general welfare of society. This development must be sustained by the government in a fair way, granting equal opportunities without distinction of class or privileges. It is important to highlight that equal opportunities do not mean that all students will obtain the same results, but that each of them will be able to develop their personal potential with the constant support of an educational program that detects their strengths and empowers them as a human being. A strengthened society, with a population educated in different fields, enriches the results, through the coordination of a resourceful society. There is no better approach to education than curiosity. Supporting individual tutoring for school students may encourage their interest in certain topics. Diversity could become a competitive advantage in the process of integration into the global value-added chain. An equitable society is one that takes care of all its children as its own children, without distinction of privileges and with the same respect that all kids deserve.

# Part II

# HOW TO OVERCOME ARGENTINE FINANCIAL CRISIS?

*September, 2018*

*After the rate exchange instability of August 2018, the government took measures to increase taxes by applying withholdings on exports. The president blamed the international "storm" for the massive capital outflow out of emerging economies, which especially hit Argentina and Turkey.*

Climatic euphemisms apart, we are facing an economic crisis. In the media, there is a tendency to criticize public spending since, as Mr. President mentioned, "we cannot spend more than we collect." However, within the 2018 budget, 76% of total expenditure was allocated to social services (payment of health pensions, retirement pensions, family allowances, son allowances, education and culture, health and social assistance) (Presidency of the Nation, 2018). We agree that it is necessary to detect those areas of the budget where savings can be achieved, but it is also necessary to note that the vast majority of these items are sensitive, and cutting them would negatively affect the social situation. Argentina is not managing abundance, but surviving in shortages.

But then, if public spending is so delicate and cannot be significantly reduced, what is the alternative? It is to collect more. This is the reason why the last economic measures pronounced after the bank run that carried our currency above $ 40 / USD were in this direction, increasing export withholdings. How much additional tax burden can be demanded from the private sector, overloaded with taxes? Not much, since this policy reduces international competitiveness and transforms economic projects into unfeasible. What is the alternative? Encourage external investment in the country, in order to increase the number of companies that pay taxes; increase employment, so employees contribute to social security (the highest income the government has, to face their budget, with a total weight of 37% of total income); and increase collections from the commercial activity accordingly, accompanying the rise in the level of employment and the revival in consumption (VAT is the second largest income in the budget, contributing approximately 20% of national resources) (Presidency of the Nation, 2018 ).

The government initially opted to attract foreign investments through trust, but never managed to do so. Why? It would seem by then that apathetic attempts to incentive development focused on agriculture and promoting local industry. But this promotion of local industry never works in Argentina. The reason is that local workforce is expensive in relation to the (misery) wages of the region (Schteingart, 2018a, 2018b). And because of the high cost it represents for the companies, it does not offer competitive technological advantages, nor skilled labour (this can be seen in the 2010 Census, where 61% of adults over 20 years old answered they had not finished high school), nor differential value added. The biggest sin of Argentina is to believe that "export" is pure property and exclusively characteristic of industrial goods.

That is why the government, when faced with the continuous devaluations that we will address in a moment, does not show any interest in recomposing the salaries of the population at the same rate (Di Santi, 2018). In his eagerness to create an export policy, it believes that lowering production costs to compete with the (misery) wages in the region and fostering labour flexibility will attract investments. However, my forecast is that it will only bring social unrest and poverty.

Returning to the question of devaluations, the diagnosis for me is clear: we have a currency crisis. As we have seen, there are no capital inflows to the country in order to buy Argentine pesos in a productive investment. The only alternative offered by this government is to promise high interest rates, with the hope that financial investments will provide the necessary dollars in the short term (Slipczuk, 2018a, 2018b). But if productive investments do not enter, as speculative capital flees (Fernandez Blanco, 2018), Argentina's sole destiny is to disappear in a whirlwind like Macondo, in an endless devaluation and hyperinflationary spiral. It is worth noting that the only moments in which Argentina did not have a crisis, were those in which foreign capital inflows arrived, namely: a) in the 1990s when state companies were privatized, stability lasted until the resources generated in this transaction were exhausted and b) With *Kirchnerism*, when agriculture generated extraordinary income and foreign inflows, stability also lasted until these resources were exhausted.

What is the economic miracle that could save this blessed land? Attracting foreign investments. What can we offer to the world today? What activities can keep the purchasing power of Argentines high? Popular knowledge often criticizes the lack of engineers. Instead, it maintains that there are plenty of professionals in other fields. There are plenty of graduates in the different branches of economic sciences. There are plenty of lawyers. There are plenty of human resources students. There are plenty of designers. There are plenty of IT students. There are plenty of people who speak foreign languages. Does Argentina have professionals in these areas to spare? The financial services centres were transformed into an economic activity that proliferates around the world (IFS2020: A Strategy for Ireland's International Financial Services sector 2015-2020, 2015). Legal advisors are now expanding, developing their activities in various latitudes to advice at the regional level. Human resources services can now be exported, since all the continent's services can be centralized in a single city, favouring the efficiency of multinationals. Design, in almost all its forms, is a fantastic tool for creating added value that can be exported all over the world. Knowledge-based activities are being developed across the globe, and it is a unique opportunity for the Argentine Republic (Alquimiaseconomicas, 2018). Distances and borders disappear, which is a matchless opportunity due to our geographical disadvantage. Argentina's strength in this new scenario is the solid local university offer. The supply of professionals in the labour market is extensive, and we currently find a greater population of graduates in these careers than available jobs.

The Argentine problem is not the shortage of engineers. The problem is the lack of public policies that foster greater diversity of knowledge-based activities, with a wide potential for insertion into the global value added chain. What can the current government do to avoid an economic crisis that seems inevitable? The open proposal from this space is to offer a tax benefit - like that of Ireland, which used this same strategy with overwhelming success - of a 12.5% income tax rate to favour the arrival of productive investments to the country. Ideally, additional benefits can be articulated, for instance, to all investments established within a one-kilometre radius of any university, in order to encourage skilled labour to be more likely to find a job, and to favour a synergy among professionals in the country and foreign investments. But is the strategy of tax-exception to companies desirable? Yes, because according to the National Budget initially analysed, more funds are raised by increasing the level of activity and the level of employment, rather than increasing the tax burden that falls on existing companies, which would otherwise prefer to enter the financial market before investing in productive areas.

The advantage of favouring the services sector is the possibility of immediate setting up of this type of organizations, which, when their demands of professionals that contribute a high added value to the global value chain are satisfied, ensure a long-term plan that guarantees their stay.

What about industry? Can these policies harm it? Not at all. My personal stand is that industry will never be the starting point of the country's economy, because in addition to requiring longer deadlines to specify its installation and setting up, it is an activity that globally lean towards one of the following two options: either it differentiates by hiring low-skilled and low-cost labour (as is the case in many countries throughout Latin America), or it seeks high added value provided by a qualified population (Germany). It is difficult, then, for the industry to be the starting point of economic recovery in the short term. What can happen is that if the country becomes an attractive economy for foreign investment and export of services, the industry is likely to grow in tune with the greater purchasing power of the population and the consequent economic development. A higher level of activity and aggregate demand can work as an engine to empower a sector that can greatly benefit from the improvement of its internal market. Attracting investments that occupy skilled labour have a multiplier effect on the economy because of the greater willingness to consume, of professionals who get a good job, generating a virtuous circle for the definitive development of a country.

# Can education explain argentine recurrent crises?

*November, 2018*

*Two completely opposite economic models followed in recent decades, failing to generate economic growth and eradicate the country's poverty. What is the main reason for this stagnation? An extended analysis of the Argentine economy tells us that it originates in the post-war stage, with ups and downs, but always returning to the same level.*

Argentina: a country condemned to success that permanently fails. A country with all the conditions to grow, dejected by its economic misadventures. A collective unconscious that longs for history books, those who point out that we were once a world powerhouse. How to explain this cyclothymia? We seek answers in political parties, in ideologies, in our currency, in foreign influences, and we resign ourselves to the idea that we are permanently mistaken. We sigh, as we want to understand how our destiny could have been so truncated. It happens to all of us. But if our goal is to understand Argentine society in greater depth, we need a well-defined context to start with.

First, 61% of adults over the age of 20 responded during the 2010 Census that they had not completed high school. Regarding school enrolment, the Ministry of Education data shows that approximately 70% of children in primary and secondary school attend public education establishments, while the remaining 30% (approx.) of enrolment is concentrated in privately managed schools («Educational Statistics», 2018). The main difference between both models lies in the attainment level, which results in a promising 62% in private education institutions and a 32% lapidary in public school (CEA - UB, 2016).

To have a global reference, in South Korea the high-school graduation rate is 98% among adults 25 to 34 years of age (OECD, 2017b, p. 44). In the same age range, 70% of South Koreans have a university degree, representing the highest percentage of OECD member countries. This is a country that at the end of World War II was plunged into poverty and social conflict after 35 years of Japanese occupation, devastated by the war with its northern neighbour, forcing the then languid South Korean economy to survive on the basis of international humanitarian aid, in order to cover its national budget. It is well-known in those latitudes, that it was the strong focus on education and work that allowed the construction of the fourteenth global economy they have today. Another economy that manages to obtain excellent indicators in its educational system is Canada, where 93% of adults between 25-34 years of age manage to finish high school and 61% achieve a bachelor's degree. The Nordic countries, Switzerland and Ireland share a school graduation rate of the order of 90%, which later results in a level of 40-50% of the population moving forward to achieve a tertiary education degree.

But, while it seems intuitive that education is a positive factor, how can it affect household's economy? The importance of these data is vital to understand the socioeconomic structure of a country, since the degree of education attainment has a direct relation with future income. According to the report "Poverty and income inequality in the urban area 2010-2017" prepared by UCA's Observatory of the Social Debt, 32% of households where the head of family without full secondary are below the poverty line, while those where he/she has completed secondary education, the percentage is reduced to

9.7%. This characteristic is replicated in households under the extreme poverty line, where 7.4% of them in which the head of the family did not complete school studies are affected by this situation of severe vulnerability, whereas when the head of household did complete its studies, the incidence of extreme poverty sets at 1.3% (ODSA - UCA, 2017). The data is conclusive: the higher the level of studies, the lower the incidence of poverty and extreme poverty. Beyond particular cases, statistically the population that does not complete their studies is more vulnerable. If the goal is to reach zero poverty, this close relationship must take centre stage in the political scene to fulfil the promise.

But can education affect a country's economy? Argentina reached a great development at the end of the 19th century as an agro-exporting powerhouse. World wars hit the economy and trade at a global scale, but since the post-war era, the world has seen extraordinary progress that allowed poverty to decline with an economic growth never witnessed before. Our country, unfortunately, failed to take advantage of this international context, and on the contrary, was a victim of successive crises. There is plenty of bibliography about the causes of this stagnation, but we are going to address the situation with a special focus on the evolution of education, and its parallelism with the economic decline suffered.

The National Constitution of 1853 forced the provinces to provide public, secular and free primary education, which was complying with different provincial regulations in subsequent years and had its highest point in the presidency of Domingo F. Sarmiento (1868 to 1874) through a strong commitment to the national school to eliminate the high illiteracy rates of the time, which reached four-fifths of the population. The Argentine economic boom notoriously concured not only with the years of free-trade incentives, but also with the years after this inclusive education policy.

Nevertheless, the Catholic Church by no means resigned its struggle to be the main educator, and with the arrival of the immigration waves, it had a strategic, as well as improvised ally: associativism, and the institutions that concentrated immigrants according to their roots, founded to keep their traditions alive, and as a meeting point. This is the reason why there were only 7.2% of primary school students attending private institutions in 1940 (historical minimum), but an enrolment that increased to 30% of students for secondary school (not yet regulated as mandatory, and therefore, relegated to political priorities) (Gamallo, 2015).

Peronism, ironically, repelled from the public school environment a society sector annoyed by the political abuse of reinforcing political ideology in textbooks, infiltrating political ideology in the classroom. Primary enrolment gradually migrated to private institutions, reaching almost 10% of the total. Through the law 13.047 of 1947, a legal framework was provided to private education, with the proviso that the secondary degrees obtained in these houses of study had yet to be validated by national authorities. It was not until 1960, by A. Frondizi, that Argentine private education - through the constant claim, especially from the Church - obtained the authority to issue qualifying titles of national validity (Gamallo, 2015).

The presidency of Frondizi had another milestone that needs to be highlighted, as it would mark a turning point in the history of Argentine education: the 1958 Teacher Coordination Board strike that deprived the students of the Buenos Aires province of any teaching activity for a period close to one month, by claiming equal salaries with their national peers («Institutional History of the Federation of Buenos Aires Educators», 2019; Marziotta, 2018). The strike lasted from September 29, 1958 until October 21. More importantly, this would be the beginning of a long and exhausting history of strikes carried out by the teacher unions. A study of the CIPPEC of 2015 ensures that one of the main points through which throughout Latin America, there is a migration from public to private schools are the numerous teacher strikes (Rivas, 2015). Educators claim for their rights but governments in general do not give in, even to long periods of inactivity. These strikes trigger the perfect combo for the decline of the system: teachers generally have sufficient reasons to go on strike; the government knows it but is not interested in negotiating, and families choose to migrate to private institutions that ensure all schooling days. A process of privatization conscious or unconscious, but that is happening throughout the continent.

So much so, that from 1980 to 2001 there were 1,584 teacher strikes throughout the national territory (75 per year) ("In Argentina there were 1,584 teacher strikes since 1980", 2002). In the province of Buenos Aires alone, in the period between 2006 and 2016 there were 110 days without classes (Di Santi, 2017). Private enrolment in primary school went from 16% in 1980 to the current 30% of total students, with increasing social segregation (Jaume, 2011).

It is remarkable to see the correlation between the gradual increase in the percentage of students devoted to private school and the gradual Argentine economic stagnation. The review of the educational systems of Norway, Australia, Switzerland, Germany, Singapore, Denmark, Ireland, Canada, South Korea and Finland that we went through in the first part of this work shows us how quality public education is an antecedent factor economic growth. This is especially true in the cases of Singapore, South Korea and Ireland, where there was a long transition between societies overwhelmed by the social crisis, and the strong economies that we see today leading the Human Development Index. Education brings economic growth, since it generates the necessary context for foreign investments that value human capital, and through the payment of high salaries for jobs that provide high added value to the international value chain, the country grows at par of society by increasing its resources. In Argentina, on the contrary, there is a direct correlation between the growth of private education - and the consequent segregation that this condition entails - and the turbulent spiral of increasingly acute crises that Argentina suffered since the post-war era.

In summary, Argentine society is not receiving a uniform education, but instead, social segregation is increasingly accentuated. The degree of progress in the studies has a direct relationship with the vulnerability of people in terms of the probability of falling below the poverty or extreme poverty line. And there is also a certain relationship between the gradual privatization of Argentine education through strikes, and poor economic performance in the country. Of course, there are multiple factors and no miraculous solutions, but if we want to understand our society, it is necessary to examine carefully how we are educating our youngsters. Perhaps multiple causes conspired against the development of Argentina, but if the purpose is to reverse the situation, it is necessary to understand that there is no possible development without education.

# Does the voucher system in Sweden work?

*December, 2018*

*Before the end of the school year, it is important to remember the importance of education as a fundamental leveller of the possibilities of children from different environments in terms of their educational opportunities.*

Milton Friedman would become the champion of the educational voucher system in the '70s, as a liberal alternative that favoured free choice of each parent over the education of their children. Over time, different countries adopted diverse variants of this system with dissimilar results. This time we will focus the attention on the transformation that took place in Sweden, where the chosen format consisted of a voucher that "accompanies" the student by giving him a fixed amount - directly paid to the educational institution - instead of financing the schools through a pre-established budget. This voucher can be used both in state educational centres - where all children have their place secured- and those that are privately managed. The only restriction for these institutions is that they cannot charge an extra fee to families, nor reject applicants under any circumstances, being accepted by order of application. After the reform introduced by the free choice system in 1992, private management schools experienced rapid growth, from 4% of the total enrolment in 2000 to 16% today (OECD, 2017c). More than 50% of these institutions are for-profit organizations.

Previously, the education system was centralized and monopolized from the state orbit. The results obtained in the international exams were well above the OECD average in the strongest subjects, and similar to the OECD average in the worst cases. In the early 1990s, Sweden would suffer a harsh economic crisis that resolved through a shift towards market-oriented policies and the privatization of public services. The change in the educational model was, consequently, more an ideological issue than a necessity, since with the advent of neoliberal ideas, the idea that public institutions were inefficient by definition became stronger - understanding that they would be more rational and efficient in private hands-, and the expenditure of resources began to be questioned with greater strength. The first measures were aimed at decentralizing educational responsibilities by returning autonomy and decision-making capacity to municipalities. This intended to increase competition and encourage the formation of private schools. The theory provided that low quality schools would suffer the loss of their students and eventually close, thus rewarding those that best meet the demands of parents.

*Sweden's performance in PISA tests (2000-2012)*

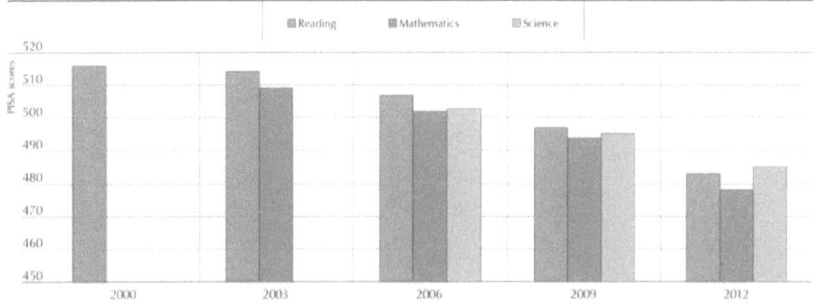

*Source: (OECD, 2015b)*

The results of the PISA exams, a global sample of the knowledge of 15-year-old students, were a blow to the country. Sweden suffered the sharpest decline in its scores among all countries evaluated between 2003 and 2012. The national debate reflected the society's concern, as it was found that a quarter of the students did not get the minimum expected score in the math tests; the quantity of outstanding students was reduced by half; and grades got worse in all evaluated areas. The most striking issue was that this evident decline had place at the same time that national measurements showed a rise in grades, an absolute contradiction not only with respect to PISA exams, but also with respect to other global tests such as TIMMS and PIRLS (OECD, 2015b ). What could be happening?

*Comparison between the average in the merit score in year 9 (15 years old) and PISA exams*

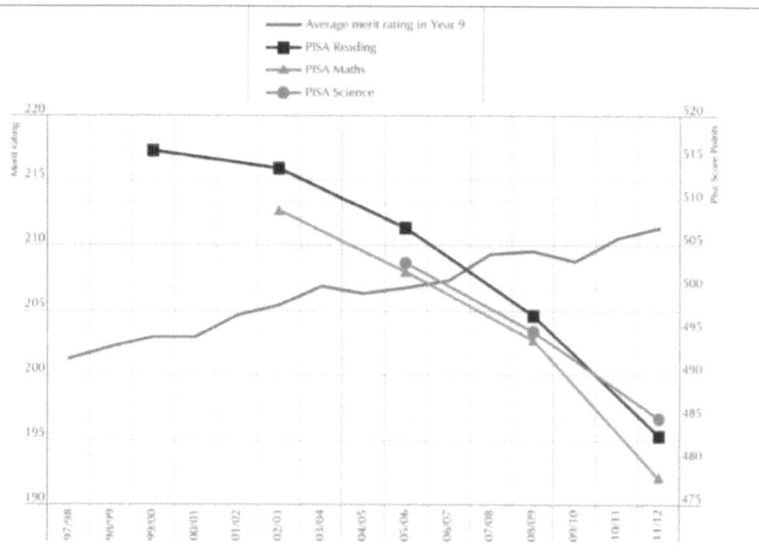

*Source: (OECD, 2015b)*

One of the main drawbacks is that the responsibility migrated from the State to the parents: they were now responsible for judging whether the education their children receive was of good or poor quality, without always having the necessary tools to do so. There are no punishments or interventions for schools, as it is "supposed" that the market will punish them. The evidence suggests that this does not happen (Butrymowicz, 2018).

Another adversity that can be found is the evaluation method: schools favour examinations with open questions that allow a high degree of subjectivity in the qualification, and in many cases teachers are pressured by school directors to grant good grades even when they do not correspond, in order to encourage parents to continue sending their children to that institution (Butrymowicz, 2018).

Schools have enough freedom to choose their own method to transmit the curriculum to students, but this emphasized the difference in results between schools. In Sweden there was a slight increase in segregation that followed the pattern of privatization. Through the introduction of free choice, society had a greater tendency to divide itself according to its social status. The index of academic inclusion fell more than in the rest of the OECD member countries in the period from 2003 to 2012. Although it remains positive, this is because the system was fully inclusive before the reform, after which it has been suffering a gradual fall. The explanation can be found in the social segmentation that is accentuated by the demographic division between neighbourhoods of immigrants and non-immigrants that emerged in the main urban centres.

In Sweden, society accepts in broad consensus that quality and equitable education is closely linked to future economic growth, which is why this situation is considered a priority issue. This is especially important for immigrants, as the government aspires to avoid increasing the cost of its welfare net, due to the large flow of asylees and refugees who arrived in recent years, who should be integrated into the Swedish economy in a productive way. In this integration, it is committed to keep attracting high value-added investments -

which demand highly qualified human resources - and reduce insecurity rates.

The voucher system is just one alternative that was implemented around the world to find the best way to educate the population. But beyond the prevailing system, it is important to understand that the main objective is to achieve a method that, through equal opportunities, enhances the economy of a country including all citizens. In this way, skilled labour has the ability to attract foreign investments of high added value that contribute to competitive wages and allow the insertion of a nation into the global value-added chain through human capital. Nothing has more value than the education of children, not only emotionally, but also economically.

# Five alternatives for preventing teachers' strike

*February, 2019*

*In the last chapter of the first part of this book we have analysed the impact of teachers' strikes on the migration from public to private schools, and the subsequent stratification that this causes. Below are five proposals aimed at mitigating this problem, focusing on the issues at stake in the beginning of the school year in the province of Buenos Aires (Argentina) during the year 2019.*

A new year starts, and so a new conflict threatens the beginning of school-year. In the Province of Buenos Aires, on the one hand, Governor Vidal argues that to negotiate salary increases, teachers have taken "students as hostages" and that they cannot "stop thinking about political intentionality, [since] they mix militancy with class days». On the other hand, the unions demand an agreement for last year's salaries before start negotiating new year's issues. The main conflict, being the high inflation rates that mined purchasing power year after year. Consequently, the unions see the inclusion of a trigger clause as non-negotiable («Teachers refused Vidal proposition», 2018). At stake, are the study days of about 2 million children.

The loss of schooling days is the main factor in the migration from public to private schools, according to a report by CIPPEC (Rivas, 2015). In fact, in the new "dialogue tables" launched by the government of María Eugenia Vidal to include parents in the educational discussion, in 88 meetings with 1200 participants, the main request was to «respect the school calendar» since parents «want classes to begin in a timely manner, expressing annoyance at the recurring loss of school days»(Santa Cruz, 2019). To offer a complete context of the political conflict scenario for this 2019, it is worth mentioning that there is a political call to affiliates of the ruling party to participate in these meetings, which puts teachers on the defensive, who feel attacked by a biased interest. The same complaint raised by Vidal against the guilds - turning the debate into a political arena- would now seem to be his strategy. Why is it "extortion" when the opponent does it, but "it is acceptable" when the government makes that same claim? The end does not justify the means, and in this chronic war of interests there will be neither victors nor vanquished, but a decline of public education quality, due to the inability of the rulers to find solutions. It is therefore very important to discuss the transparency of these meetings; provide equal representation; ensure balance in the voices that compose it; and point to objective conclusions that seek to improve the conditions of regional education. If, instead, they were used as a weapon against those already beaten -economically- teachers to erode the claim for a fair salary, the children will be affected again (Naveiro, 2019).

Currently, according to the provincial government, «initial salary of a teacher reached AR$ 16,710 [gross], while the average salary is at AR$ 32,865. And with no working-day loses it would be AR$ 17,210 and AR$ 33,365, respectively». The provincial Minister of Economy, Hernan Lacunza, emphasizes that «the salary mass for all items compensates and even has a small gain with respect to the cost of living» ("Teachers refused salary proposal", 2018). Official optimism does not prevent the comparison of this figures with the OECD member countries, being 53% below the average for the starting salaries (matching the member countries with the lowest wages) and 31% below the average salary (normalized values at purchasing power parity). Needless to say, the mentioned remunerations are below private business sector average, which undermines the attractiveness of the career for future professionals. We can find an extremely antagonistic case in Finland, where only 10% of the candidates for the study of teaching profession pass entrance admission, and those who are not allowed into a teaching career seek jobs in law or medicine. Such is the level of priority that Finnish government gives to its education, and such is the degree of status this professional career has in society (OECD Observer, 2019).

Meanwhile, the de-financing of public education in Argentina gets deeper every day. Roberto Baradel accuses Maria Eugenia Vidal of not delivering notebooks, textbooks, or even school maintenance. Echoing the information presented by Mercedes Montaña and Alejandro Morduchowicz, the gross salary of a 10-year-old grade teacher in the province of Buenos Aires without the teaching strikes would not be AR$ 20,501 - as it is today - but AR$ 8,530. If initial salary proposals were automatically accepted, teaching salary would be practically non-existent.

In this context, the political conflict in an electoral period threatens to affect the weakest: children are left without classes, their parents live in uncertainty, and in the long term it negatively affects the development of future professionals. It is necessary to find innovative and creative alternatives that change the rules of a historical and fruitless discussion.

The following are 5 alternatives so that children do not miss a day of school. 5 alternatives to give teachers a voice. 5 alternatives so that conflicts do not threaten children. 5 alternatives to build the country we wish:

*1) Grant by law a space in the media for teachers organizations, in order to inform society about the claims of the teacher struggle.*

A daily or weekly space of 50% of second page on national circulation newspapers can help give voice to teachers across the country in order to expose their differences with respect to policies, favouring a genuine debate, clear-cut and without media intermediation misrepresenting their claims. By agreeing on the information to be delivered, for instance, through a trade union assembly, this space has the ability to bring all parents an update on the teaching claims of an area as sensitive as the education of their children. In addition, it favours information and transparency.

*2) Mandatory publication of statistical data by government authorities concerning education.*

In order to avoid the politicization of this confrontation through unfounded opinions, it is a must to have clear statistics on the different edges that affect education. It is necessary that all levels of government (national and provincial) are to publish information on the real evolution of the teachers' salary; a semi-annual comparison with the countries of the region; expenditure per student and school in the public sphere, as well as in the privately managed institutions; detailed public expenses; detailed transfers to the private sector; etc.

The unions report that a 32% raise is far from annual inflation. The Minister of Economy argues that there is no loss of purchasing power. If the minister pronounces, with great certainty, that teachers did not lose purchasing power against rising prices, it should be based on genuine data. The reference indicator for this type of debate is currently published by the General Coordination of Cost Studies of the Educational System (Cgecse, dependent on the national education portfolio), which should be enriched with more data and indexes. Ideally, the pursued standard should be a set of indicators that tend to converge with those published by the OECD, in order to allow the comparison of information with international standards.

*3) Generate a space on a government website to expose the issues at stake.*

Always with the intention of giving visibility to the problems faced by teachers and possible political proposals, the claim can be democratized through a virtual space that increases the plurality of voices in the debate and informs society. This space should organize the information in such a way that teachers can express themselves and any reader can get information. Likewise, it should consider the possibility of facilitating the proposals of politicians oriented to solve the problems; and to provide present-day government to express their point of view on the situation. And not less important, such a web space would allow the consolidation of all the information dispersed in different government sites on expenses, investment, registration, different indicators of the provinces, etc.

*4) Pay indexed salaries.*

The most utopian proposal, but which would get at the root of the problem, would be to index teachers' salaries to a representative inflation index. In doing so, the discussion is neutralised due to the stabilization of the salary lose against inflation. A combination of indexed salaries and the exposure of their claims in the main national media would disrupt the strikes, by combining the security of an updated income and disclose teachers' claims, involving society in the day-to-day evolution of public education.

*5) Acknowledge investments in education as an asset.*

The public spending in highways and public infrastructure carried out in the province consume a significant portion of the available resources. If a share of this budget is allocated to school renovation, the same amount of workforce would be needed, and the student's learning environment would be improved. A high-quality building infrastructure is the minimum that government should provide.

Not only can employment be generated through the maintenance and renovation of educational institutions, but education can be used as a market itself. Taking the reference from Singapore, where teachers are entitled to 100 subsidized hours per year of training, there is the possibility of promoting the professionalization of teachers, generating employment and boosting education at a low cost. A hundred hours can be subsidized in approved private establishments, focusing in developing the teacher's necessary skills to empower the educational quality. This independent market, with trainings freely chosen by teachers, has the capacity to generate great synergy in the sector, multiplying each dollar invested in the form of knowledge, employment and improvement in student results (Stewart, 2019).

# Economic cycle in Argentina

## (Or: "Why is there an economic crisis every 10 years in Argentina?)

*April, 2019*

*Most countries in the world eradicated the curse of inflation in the 1980s after focusing its attention on monetary policy, regulating the monetary base and closely watching the primary deficit in their economies. In Argentina, money printing is a widely abused political tool, financing a public spending deficit that no politician has been able to restrain. In this chapter, we are going to analyse how money printing causes inflation in Argentina, and what is the transmission channel to prices that generates a permanent increase in prices year after year. The speed of inflation has particularities in Argentina, different from those in USA or UE, as the money loses its purchasing value at a rapid pace.*

The current issue in Argentine politics seem to be their difficulty in explaining why the economic growth of the "peronism" governments were fictional, but they lack the precise means to defend their position. If we are to try to find a precise explanation, we must begin by addressing that every inflationary process initially generates an economic stimulus. This is because when the government injects money into the economy, in the very short term, the people who beneficiates from this new money increase their consumption. In a hypothetical scenario, where we are analysing the initial moment of the general price increase, the entrepreneur, who does not know (in the very short term) the origin of the money, believes that there is a tendency of the population to choose their products. This will lead manufacturers (in the short term) to increase prices, as consumption pushes aggregate demand. As enterprises see their sales go up, they will probably hire more employees. Seeing business run smooth, other entrepreneurs are likely to offer goods or services to meet the increased aggregate demand and there is a boost in employment. Supply will increase, as entrepreneurs interpret that their business is growing.

This way, every month government injects the money that central bank just printed, and now there's plenty of money in the economy (therefore, money is now 5% more abundant, 10% more abundant, 50% more abundant as monetary base increases) it undergoes a process of value erosion with respect to foreign currencies. If this were not so, - very hypothetically - we could print argentine pesos indefinitely and buy all existing dollars in the world. But the global market does not accept this, and in order to adjust its variables, exchange rates rise sharply on the overprinted currency. This occurs when the aggregate money volume existing in local currency tries to cover its purchasing power by buying a strong foreign currency as US dollars, in order to avoid any possible stability. This, in Argentina, is so embedded in people's minds as a result of cyclical economic crises every ten years, and the experience that exchange rates go always up, so nobody ever lost purchasing power by buying US dollars in the last eighty years. As this happens, the excess of argentine pesos bid up international currencies, devaluating the local currency. This devaluation makes all production inputs "more expensive" (in pesos, because they will keep the same price in US dollars). Input price rise in argentine pesos produce an equivalent rise in sales prices, producing a generalized increase in domestic prices. This happens because goods tend to equilibrium in US dollars, so prices in local currency reflect the new exchange rate caused by the overprinted money bidding up foreign currencies. When the economic sacrifice to make a purchase in the domestic market increases, the aggregate demand decreases and the indicators that entrepreneurs believed to be favourable market signs towards his product vanish. Aggregate demand normalizes or falls. The economic situation returns to its original equilibrium and the lower demand hits the new bidders who believed that there was economic growth, causing most probably bankrupts, since if there was no place for them at the time of the original situation, there will not be any now.

Technically, the devaluation affects the speed of money (M x V = Q x P where V represents the average number of times that each monetary unit is used to make a purchase - the transactional speed of money -) by the impact of expectations. By undermining the purchasing power of each peso, nobody wants to lose purchasing power and the immediate tendency is to take refuge in a foreign currency that retains its value. It is for this reason that Argentina and Venezuela, in order to extend as long as possible the favourable situation that inflation presents when pushing aggregate demand, were forced to implement financial restrictions in the exchange market, appeasing the speed generated by the monetary issue and thus artificially obstruct the market attempt to return to its equilibrium point.

This situation is the antithesis of economic growth fostered by foreign trade, which brings supply and demand of local currency to the exchange market, encouraging genuine economic growth. If instead of printing money, investment from international capitals perform a transaction in any country, then this is new money that genuinely stimulate the economy. This international transaction is validated by the international market, encouraging economic growth. Exporting is radically different from money printing, in the sense of the validity that the international market gives to the transaction that generated the monetary liquidity. It is because of this validation that it does not generate inflation.

The above-described process of inflation as an incentive for the economy contains implicitly the concept of 'lag', or delay, intrinsic to the discovery of fluctuations by each of the economic actors. This is so true at the beginning, where we can see an apparent reactivation, as in the end, where normally - if genuine international transactions are not generated - a recession is observed. In this way, governments gladly accept receiving credit for the initial stimulus that the monetary expansion provides to the economy, but they are reluctant to admit that later the generalized price increase will absorb this initial prosperity. Once this process has begun, it is very difficult for political leaders to stop it, because it usually entails an economic decline, which is nothing more than the economy returning to its original state, on which no fundamental measure has been taken to encourage growth, and therefore it would seem that a recession occurs. The problem for politicians is that inflation is easily implemented, but it cannot be abruptly stopped.

It is for this reason that the Argentine economy suffers from a poverty that chronically punishes a third of the population: economic growth is not structural but ephemeral, dependent on the eternal inertia of the generalized price increase. The only way to modify this misfortune and eradicate poverty is through integrated trade to the rest of the world.

The key is to concentrate efforts on job creation over tax collection (withholdings, fees, taxes), since the income of resources will compensate the benefits granted.

A final word regarding price control attempts: generally, empirical evidence indicates that they are fruitless. The market will try to accommodate in one way or another. The essence of a price control program should be to solve an immediate problem in the very short term, but that requires a stimulus of the economy aimed at generating export-oriented employment to generate the necessary resources that strengthen demand and can restore prices to their breakeven point. In the words of Milton Friedman, price controls:

> «They are like putting a brick on a boiling kettle to prevent the lid from yielding. If, simultaneously, the flame under the kettle is extinguished, the brick "can prevent" this from happening. But if the flame increases, the pressure will strengthen until the lid explodes» (Butler, 1985).

That is, inflation will probably explode if a set of preventive measures that accompany such control are not taken.

# Fibonacci taxation

*August, 2019*

*The closure of small and medium enterprises is a typical characteristic of the process analysed in the previous article, in which the inflationary inertia must come to an end in an orderly manner or out of control through a hyperinflationary spiral. The bankrupt of companies is daily, and the stimulation of exports has no immediate results. To mitigate the consequences of these cycles, a tax system is proposed, that relieves the burden on companies in vulnerable situations and on people who lose purchasing power during the financial adjustment of the national economy.*

    The tax issue currently divides opinions. For some, taxes are the best way to redistribute an excessive income in top earners, while others favour a low tax burden that stimulates job creation to boost development. The victims are always the same: on the one hand, the small and medium-sized companies that are drowned by the tax burden, and on the other, the working middle class whose income is diminished by their collaboration with the exchequer, which does not provide services according to the economic sacrifice. Taxes become a heavy burden, preventing the growth of businesses and people. But is there perhaps a precise formula to grow?

    The sequence of numbers known as 'Fibonacci' is closely linked to the golden number: a mathematical expression of unique characteristics, which is found repeatedly in nature as a growth formula that allows the most efficient development of numerous species of plants. The leaves that grow around a stem, the sunflower flower seeds, and the conifer pineapples are all examples of how nature found in mathematics a harmonious and perfect form of development.

Leonardo de Pisa, better known by his nickname Fibonacci, an abbreviation of filius Bonacci - son of Bonacci - was an Italian mathematician to whom we not only owe this numerical succession thanks to his book Liber Abbaci of 1202, but also, thanks to his work, the Indo-Arabic numbering system - that is, the numbers we currently use - began to be used in Europe. The sequence consists of adding the two previous numbers to form a new one, assuming that we begin with 0 and 1. Thus, the - infinite - sequence begins as follows:

$$0 + 1 = 1$$
$$1 + 1 = 2$$
$$2 + 1 = 3$$
$$3 + 2 = 5$$
$$5 + 3 = 8$$
$$8 + 5 = 13$$
$$13 + 8 = 21$$
$$21 + 13 = 34$$
$$34 + 21 = 55$$
$$55 + 34 = 89$$
$$89 + 55 = 144$$
$$144 + 89 = 233$$
$$233 + 144 = 377$$
$$377 + 233 = 610$$
$$610 + 377 = 987$$
$$987 + 610 = 1,597$$
$$1,597 + 987 = 4,181$$

$$4{,}181 + 1{,}597 = 6{,}765$$
$$6{,}765 + 4{,}181 = 10{,}946$$
$$10{,}946 + 6{,}765 = 17{,}711$$
$$17{,}711 + 10{,}946 = 28{,}657$$
$$28{,}657 + 17{,}711 = 46{,}368$$
$$46{,}368 + 28{,}657 = 75{,}025$$

If this sequence indicates a pattern of nature for a balanced growth, is it possible to use it for the development of people, or of economic activity? Is there a tax system that can be fair and adequate for all members of society?

Thanks to its mathematical properties, one of its greatest virtues is flexibility: an increase of one percentage point can be assigned to each jump in the sequence, or two percentage points, or five, etc. In addition, the maximum limit can be established according to the economic objectives of any given government (such as 20%, 24%, 30%), and an early cut of the maximum rate in the economic sectors to be favoured (for example, a maximum limit of 12% for the export of knowledge-based services).

In this way, two or three options can be adopted, one for companies, another for employees and another for freelancers. For instance:

- Companies can be taxed (we refer here to Income Tax) with a scale that increases by two percentage points for every step in net income, fostering the development of SMEs. A possible taxation could be the following:

- Monthly profit up to $1 thousand, would pay 2% income tax
- Monthly profit up to $2 thousand, would pay 4% income tax
- Monthly profit up to $3 thousand, would pay 6% income tax
- Monthly profit up to $5 thousand, would pay 8% income tax
- Monthly profit up to $8 thousand, would pay 10% income tax
- Monthly profit up to $13 thousand, would pay 12% income tax
- Monthly profit up to $21 thousand, would pay 14% income tax
- Monthly profit up to $34 thousand, would pay 16% income tax
- Monthly profit up to $55 thousand, would pay 18% income tax
- Monthly profit up to $89 thousand, would pay 20% income tax
- Monthly profit up to $144 thousand, would pay 22% income tax
- Monthly profit up to $233 thousand, would pay 24% income tax
- Monthly profit over $377 thousand would pay 26% income tax

This has two benefits. On the one hand, it allows SMEs to reinvest their profits to expand, and at the same time allows them to always have a fair rate according to the obtained economic results. On the other hand, large companies do not face an excessive burden in periods of losses or heavy investment, ensuring adequate compensation for the rest of the periods with a regular profit.

- A salaried worker would pay:

- Annual gross salary from $24,000 would pay a 5% tax rate
- Annual gross salary from $48,000 would pay a 8% tax rate
- Annual gross salary from $72,000 would pay a 13% tax rate
- Annual gross salary from $96,000 would pay a 21% tax rate
- Annual gross salary from $120,000 would pay a 34% tax rate

Finally, for the self-employed, a scale similar to that applied for companies can be created, but applying a rate of one fifth of the amount mentioned above:
- A self-employed earning:

- Monthly income up to $1 thousand, would pay a 8% tax rate
- Monthly income up to $1,6 thousand, would pay a 10% tax rate
- Monthly income up to $2,6 thousands, would pay a 12% tax rate

- Monthly income up to $4,2 thousands, would pay a 14% tax rate
- Monthly income up to $6,8 thousands, would pay a 16% tax rate
- Monthly income up to $11 thousands, would pay a 18% tax rate
- Monthly income up to $17,8 thousands, would pay a 20% tax rate
- Monthly income up to $28,8 thousands, would pay a 22% tax rate
- Monthly income up to $46,6 thousands, would pay a 24% tax rate
- Monthly income over $75,4 thousands would pay a 26% tax rate

A tax system that is perceived as fair by society increases collection since it avoids evasion. This is the case of the Nordic countries, in which the high tax burden that falls on individuals is seen as a necessary contribution to maintain the education and health systems that protect the population. The problem with the scales currently used lies in the proportionally greater participation suffered by lower income sectors, impeding their growth and development. A spiral-based incremental system contributes to the equal opportunities of society, and in the long term it will surely generate a greater amount of resources for the nation.

# Bibliography

Aaron E. Carroll, A. F. (2017, October 2). What Makes Singapore's Health Care So Cheap? *The New York Times*. Retrieved from https://www.nytimes.com/2017/10/02/upshot/what-makes-singapores-health-care-so-cheap.html

Alquimiaseconomicas, ~. (2018, February 14). ¿Son los servicios el futuro del desarrollo productivo en la Argentina? Retrieved 24 September 2019, from ALQUIMIAS ECONÓMICAS website: https://alquimiaseconomicas.com/2018/02/14/son-los-servicios-el-futuro-del-desarrollo-productivo-en-la-argentina/

Amanda Coletta. (2018, February 23). Canada's health-care system is a point of national pride. But a study shows it's at risk of becoming outdated. Retrieved 23 September 2019, from Washington Post website: https%3A%2F%2Fwww.washingtonpost.com%2Fnews%2Fwo rldviews%2Fwp%2F2018%2F02%2F23%2Fcanadas-health-care-system-is-a-point-of-national-pride-but-a-study-shows-it-might-be-stalled%2F

Barro, R. (1998). The East Asian Tigers Have Plenty to Roar About. *Business Week.*

BBC Mundo. (2015). Lee Kuan Yew, el hombre que convirtió a Singapur en una potencia económica. Retrieved 23 September 2019, from BBC News Mundo website: https://www.bbc.com/mundo/noticias/2015/03/150323_singapur_lee_kuan_yew_jm

Butler, E. (1985). *Milton Friedman: A guide to his economic thought.* New York: Universe Books.

Butrymowicz, S. (2018, February 28). Is Sweden proof that school choice doesn't improve education? Retrieved 24 September 2019, from PBS NewsHour website: https://www.pbs.org/newshour/education/is-sweden-proof-that-school-choice-doesnt-improve-education

CEA - UB. (2016). Lejos de la igualdad de oportunidades en la escuela secundaria. *Centro de Estudios de La Universidad de Belgrano*, (52), 16.

Cubberley, Ellwood P. (1920). *The History of Education*. Boston: Houghton Mifflin Company.

Deloitte. (2015). *Deloitte: Taxation and Investment in Switzerland 2015*. Retrieved from Deloitte website: https://www2.deloitte.com/content/dam/Deloitte/global/Documents/Tax/dttl-tax-switzerlandguide-2015.pdf

Deloitte. (2017). *Deloitte: Taxation and Investment in Canada 2017*. Retrieved from Deloitte website: https://www2.deloitte.com/content/dam/Deloitte/global/Documents/Tax/dttl-tax-canadaguide-2017.pdf

Deloitte. (2018a). *International Tax – Denmark Highlights 2018*. Retrieved from Deloitte website: https://www2.deloitte.com/content/dam/Deloitte/global/Documents/Tax/dttl-tax-denmarkhighlights-2019.pdf

Deloitte. (2018b). *Working and living in Denmark*. Retrieved from Deloitte website: https://www2.deloitte.com/content/dam/Deloitte/dk/Documents/tax/Downloads/Deloitte-Working-living-in-Denmark-2019.pdf

Department of Foreign Affairs and Trade. (2017). *The Australian Education System*. Retrieved from https://dfat.gov.au/aid/topics/investment-priorities/education-health/education/Documents/australian-education-system-foundation.pdf

Department of Foreign Affairs and Trade. (2019). Trade liberalisation and economic reform. Retrieved 22 September 2019, from Department of Foreign Affairs and Trade website: http://dfat.gov.au/about-australia/australia-world/Pages/trade.aspx

Di Santi, M. (2017, March 6). Vidal: "En los últimos diez años hemos tenido más de 110 días de paro". Retrieved 24 September 2019, from Chequeado website: https://chequeado.com/ultimas-noticias/vidal-en-los-ultimos-diez-anos-hemos-tenido-mas-de-110-dias-de-paro/

Di Santi, M. (2018, September 6). El Gobierno anunció medidas para reforzar la cobertura social: Cómo evolucionaron los planes sociales, la AUH y las jubilaciones. Retrieved 24 September 2019, from Chequeado website: https://chequeado.com/el-explicador/el-gobierno-anuncio-medidas-para-reforzar-la-cobertura-social-como-evolucionaron-los-planes-sociales-la-auh-y-las-jubilaciones/

Docentes rechazaron suba de Vidal. (2018, November 29). Retrieved 24 September 2019, from Ambito Financiero website: https://www.ambito.com/docentes-rechazaron-suba-vidal-igual-les-pagara-bono-7-mil-copy-n5002292

En la Argentina hubo 1.584 paros docentes desde 1980. (2002, March 13). Retrieved 24 September 2019, from Centro de Estudios Nueva Mayoría website: http://www.nuevamayoria.com/invest/sociolab/csola130302.htm

Estadística Educativa. (2018, April 6). Retrieved 24 September 2019, from Argentina.gob.ar website: https://www.argentina.gob.ar/educacion/planeamiento/info-estadistica/educativa

Europe: Finland—The World Factbook—Central Intelligence Agency. (2019). Retrieved 23 September 2019, from https://www.cia.gov/library/publications/the-world-factbook/geos/fi.html

Europe: Germany—The World Factbook—Central Intelligence Agency. (2019). Retrieved 23 September 2019, from https://www.cia.gov/library/publications/the-world-factbook/geos/gm.html

Europe: Norway—The World Factbook—Central Intelligence Agency. (2019). Retrieved 22 September 2019, from https://www.cia.gov/library/publications/the-world-factbook/geos/no.html

FactCheck: Does Ireland really have the 'highest education' in Europe? (2016). Retrieved 23 September 2019, from https://www.thejournal.ie/ireland-european-education-rankings-facts-eoghan-murphy-cnbc-2992092-Sep2016/

Fernandez Blanco, P. (2018, August 30). Quién compra dólares en la Argentina. Retrieved 24 September 2019, from https://www.lanacion.com.ar/economia/dolar/quien-compra-dolares-argentina-nid2167194

Gamallo, G. (2015). La 'publificación' de las escuelas privadas en Argentina. *Revista SAAP, 9*(1), 43–74.

Gapminder Foundation. (2015). *GDP, PPP (constant 2005 international $)*. Retrieved from https://docs.google.com/spreadsheets/d/16rpYapnUDKQXJI dUT_QWuuYH83dLBgbFQC3GfRO8OQY/pub#

Goh Chor Boon, S. G. (2006). *The Development of Education in Singapore since 1965*. Retrieved from https://pdfs.semanticscholar.org/c528/f7851df53fc7ac210ea ec0a8042946f43663.pdf

Health Consumer Powerhouse. (2015). *Euro health consumer index. 2015*. Retrieved from https://healthpowerhouse.com/media/EHCI-2017/EHCI-2017-report.pdf

*Healthcare in Denmark: An overview*. (2016). Ministry of Health.

Historia Institucional de la Federación de Educadores Bonaerenses FEB. (2019). Retrieved 24 September 2019, from Federación de Educadores Bonaerenses FEB website: http://feb.org.ar/institucional/historia

*IFS2020: A Strategy for Ireland's International Financial Services sector 2015-2020*. (2015). Retrieved from https://assets.gov.ie/5949/230119134451-7323c03dfe3f4ca4a2b55e4737eb498c.pdf

IMF. (2019a). Net lending/borrowing (Gen. Govt.) as percent of GDP (Norway). Retrieved 22 September 2019, from IMF Data—Acces to macroeconomic & Financial data website: https://data.imf.org/?sk=061a17b2-7e6a-4b58-9b17-042af9e59a3d&sId=1390030109571

IMF. (2019b, April). World Economic Outlook (April 2019)—Implied PPP conversion rate. Retrieved 24 September 2019, from https://www.imf.org/external/datamapper/PPPEX@WEO

Islam, S. C., Faisal. (2017, August 2). How Canada became an education superpower. *BBC News*. Retrieved from https://www.bbc.com/news/business-40708421

Jaume, D. J. (2011). *Evolución de la segregación escolar en Argentina* (Tesis de Maestría, Universidad Nacional de La Plata). Retrieved from

http://sedici.unlp.edu.ar/bitstream/handle/10915/18221/Do

cumento_completo.pdf?sequence=3

KPMG. (2016). *Clarity on Business Location Switzerland*. Retrieved

from KPMG website:

https://assets.kpmg/content/dam/kpmg/ch/pdf/clarity-on-

business-location-switzerland-en.pdf

KPMG. (2019). *Clarity on Swiss Taxes*. Retrieved from KPMG website:

https://assets.kpmg/content/dam/kpmg/ch/pdf/clarity-on-

swiss-taxes-2019-en.pdf

Kuhnle, Stein, H., Sven E. O. (2004). *The Developmental Welfare State*

*in Scandinavia: Lessons for the Developing World* (No. ISSN

1020-8208; p. 34). Retrieved from United Nations Research

Institute for Social Development website:

https://www.files.ethz.ch/isn/102834/17.pdf

Marziotta, G. (2018, April 18). 1881-2018: La historia sin fin de los

paros docentes. Retrieved 24 September 2019, from Infobae

website:

https://www.infobae.com/opinion/2018/04/18/1881-2018-la-historia-sin-fin-de-los-paros-docentes/

Milne, R. S., & Mauzy, D. K. (1990). *Singapore: The legacy of Lee Kuan Yew*. Boulder: Westview Press.

Ministry of Education and Science. (2004). *A Brief Description Of the Irish Education System*. Retrieved from https://www.education.ie/en/Publications/Education-Reports/A-Brief-Description-of-the-Irish-Education-System.pdf

Ministry of Finance, Norway. (2018, May 15). Stronger growth, lower unemployment and a more sustainable welfare state [Pressemelding]. Retrieved 22 September 2019, from Government.no website: https://www.regjeringen.no/en/aktuelt/revised-budget-2018-stronger-growth-lower-unemployment-and-a-more-sustainable-welfare-state/id2601295/

Ministry of Higher Education and Science. (2019). The State Education Grant and Loan Scheme in Denmark (SU)—Uddannelses- og Forskningsministeriet [Page]. Retrieved 23 September 2019, from https://ufm.dk/en/education/grants-and-loans/su-2013-the-danish-student-s-grants-and-loans-scheme

Naveiro, J. (2019, February 3). Vidal prepara una campaña para presionar a los docentes antes del inicio de las clases. Retrieved 24 September 2019, from https://www.tiempoar.com.ar/nota/vidal-prepara-una-campana-para-presionar-a-los-docentes-antes-del-inicio-de-las-clases

Norges Bank. (2019). About the Government Pension Fund Global. Retrieved 22 September 2019, from Norges Bank Investment Management website: https://www.nbim.no/en/the-fund/about-the-fund/

North America: Canada—The World Factbook—Central Intelligence

Agency. (2019). Retrieved 23 September 2019, from

https://www.cia.gov/library/publications/the-world-

factbook/geos/ca.html

ODSA - UCA. (2017). *Pobreza y desigualdad por ingresos en la*

*Argentina urbana 2010-2017* (p. 28). Retrieved from

Pontificia Universidad Católica Argentina website:

http://wadmin.uca.edu.ar/public/ckeditor/2017-

Observatorio-Informe-pobreza-por-Ingresos-Final.pdf

OECD. (2014). *Education Policy Outlook Denmark*. Retrieved from

http://www.oecd.org/education/EDUCATION%20POLICY%20

OUTLOOK%20DENMARK_EN.pdf

OECD. (2015a). *Education Policy Outlook 2015*. Retrieved from

https://www.oecd-

ilibrary.org/content/publication/9789264225442-en

OECD. (2015b). *Improving Schools in Sweden: An OECD Perspective*.

Retrieved from OECD website:

http://www.oecd.org/education/school/Improving-Schools-in-Sweden.pdf

OECD. (2016). *OECD Economic Surveys: Korea 2016*. Retrieved from https://www.oecd-ilibrary.org/content/publication/eco_surveys-kor-2016-en

OECD. (2017a). *Better Life Initiative—Country note Canada*. Retrieved from OECD website: https://www.oecd.org/statistics/Better-Life-Initiative-country-note-Canada.pdf

OECD. (2017b). *Education at a Glance 2017. OECD Indicators*. Retrieved from https://www.oecd-ilibrary.org/content/publication/eag-2017-en

OECD. (2017c). *School choice and school vouchers: An OECD perspective*. Retrieved from OECD website: http://www.oecd.org/education/School-choice-and-school-vouchers-an-OECD-perspective.pdf

OECD. (2019). Health spending (indicator). https://doi.org/10.1787/8643de7e-en

OECD Observer. (2019, January). The secret to Finnish education: Trust. Retrieved 24 September 2019, from http://oecdobserver.org/news/fullstory.php/aid/6126/The_secret_to_Finnish_education:_Trust.html

Oey, Alexander. (2012). The German economic model. In *The German economic model*. Retrieved from https://www.youtube.com/watch?v=jOFHpyoXsD4

Office of the United States Trade Representative. (2015). *2015 National Trade Estimate Report on Foreign Trade Barriers*. Washington, D.C.

Presidencia de la Nación. (2018). Presupuesto Ciudadano 2018. Retrieved 24 September 2019, from pagina-area.html

Puiggrós, A. (2015). *Imperialismo y educación en América Latina* (Edición corregida y ampliada). Buenos Aires, Argentina: Colihue.

PwC. (2019). Switzerland—Taxes on personal income. Retrieved 23 September 2019, from http://taxsummaries.pwc.com/uk/taxsummaries/wwts.nsf/I

D/Switzerland-Individual-Taxes-on-personal-income

Rick Noack. (2015, February 4). Why Danish students are paid to go to college. *The Washington Post*. Retrieved from https://www.washingtonpost.com/news/worldviews/wp/2015/02/04/why-danish-students-are-paid-to-go-to-college/

Rivas, A. (2015). *América Latina después de PISA: Lecciones aprendidas de la educación en siete países (2000-2015)*. Buenos Aires, Argentina: CIPPEC.

Santa Cruz, D. (2019, February 4). Vidal incorpora a los padres al debate docente con mesas de diálogo. Retrieved 24 September 2019, from https://www.lanacion.com.ar/politica/vidal-incorpora-a-los-padres-al-debate-docente-con-mesas-de-dialogo-nid2216976

Schteingart, D. (2018a, June 26). El rompecabezas del mercado laboral latinoamericano | Nueva Sociedad. Retrieved 24 September 2019, from Nueva Sociedad | Democracia y política en América Latina website:

http://nuso.org/articulo/el-rompecabezas-del-mercado-laboral-latinoamericano/

Schteingart, D. (2018b, July 9). Camaño, sobre el salario mínimo: "En el ranking de asalariados en dólares de la región hoy estamos cuartos". Retrieved 24 September 2019, from Chequeado website: https://chequeado.com/ultimas-noticias/camano-sobre-el-salario-minimo-en-el-ranking-de-asalariados-en-dolares-de-la-region-hoy-estamos-cuartos/

Sclafani, Susan. (2008). *Rethinking Human Capital in Education: Singapore As A Model for Teacher Development* (p. 25). Retrieved from The Aspen Institute website: https://assets.aspeninstitute.org/content/uploads/files/content/docs/education/SingaporeEDU.pdf

Shackleton, D. F. (1975). *Tommy Douglas*. Toronto: McClelland and Stewart.

Slipczuk, M. (2018a, May 15). Qué son las Lebacs y por qué son importantes. Retrieved 24 September 2019, from Chequeado website: https://chequeado.com/el-explicador/que-son-las-lebacs-y-por-que-la-licitacion-de-manana-es-importante/

Slipczuk, M. (2018b, August 30). ¿Qué significa que el Banco Central haya subido la tasa de interés al 60%? Retrieved 24 September 2019, from Chequeado website: https://chequeado.com/el-explicador/que-significa-que-el-banco-central-haya-subido-la-tasa-de-interes-al-60/

Statistics Norway. (2016). *Facts about education in Norway 2017—Key figures 2015* (p. 36). Retrieved from https://www.ssb.no/en/utdanning/artikler-og-publikasjoner/_attachment/287176?_ts=158d834b638

Stewart, V. (2019). How Singapore Developed a High-Quality Teacher Workforce. Retrieved 24 September 2019, from Asia Society website: https://asiasociety.org/global-cities-education-network/how-singapore-developed-high-quality-teacher-workforce

Swiss Coordination Centre for Research in Education. (2014). *Swiss Education Report*. Retrieved from Swiss Coordination Centre for Research in Education website: http://skbf-csre.ch/fileadmin/files/pdf/bildungsmonitoring/Swiss_Education_Report_2014.pdf

The Commonwealth Fund. (2017). *International Profiles of Health Care Systems*. Retrieved from The Commonwealth Fund website: https://www.commonwealthfund.org/sites/default/files/documents/___media_files_publications_fund_report_2017_may_mossialos_intl_profiles_v5.pdf

The Ministry of Higher Education and Science, The Ministry for Children, Education and Gender Equality, & The Ministry of Culture. (2016). *The Danish Education System*. Retrieved from http://hfc.dk/media/252204/the_danish_education_system_pdfa.pdf

Tong, Y. T., Sheela Narayanan, & Paul, P. (2015). *Caring for our people: 50 years of healthcare in Singapore.*

Wizenberg, D., & Varsavsky, J. (2017). *Corea: Dos caras extremas de una misma nación.*

World Bank (Ed.). (1993). *The East Asian miracle: Economic growth and public policy.* New York, N.Y: Oxford University Press.

Yergin, Daniel, S., Joseph. (2002). The Commanding Heights. In *Episode 1: The Battle of Ideas.* Retrieved from http://www.pbs.org/wgbh/commandingheights/hi/index.html

# Index

**"**

"The Troubles", 57

**1**

1960s, 13, 20, 31, 43, 58, 61, 75
1970s, 41, 59, 76, 84
1980s, 21, 59, 83, 133
1990s, 58, 59, 76, 83, 86, 105, 119
19th, 8, 112

**2**

20th, 8, 14, 50, 57, 58

**7**

70s, 13, 38, 43, 49, 118

**'**

'80s, 76

**A**

Andreas Schleicher, 67
Argentina, 2, 11, 29, 75, 91, 92, 93, 94, 95, 96, 97, 103, 104, 105, 106, 110, 112, 114, 115, 116, 125, 127, 132, 133, 134, 135, 145, 150, 151, 153, 157, 159, 160

Asian Tigers, 74, 76, 146
Australia, 10, 19

**B**

Belgium, 38, 82
Berlin Wall, 33, 39, 84
Brexit, 62

**C**

Canada, 10, 64, 65, 67, 69, 70, 71, 111, 115, 145, 147, 153, 157, 158
Catholic, 8, 9, 36, 37, 113
Celtic Tiger, 62

**Ch**

Charles Haughey, 59
Chile, 22, 67, 92, 97
China, 20, 22, 38, 73

**C**

Colombia, 92
Costa Rica, 67

**D**

Denmark, 10, 13, 15, 38, 49, 50, 51, 53, 54, 62, 88, 115, 147, 148, 152, 156, 157
Douglas, Tommy, 68

## E

educación, 1
EFTA, 26
England, 8, 53
Enlightenment, 7, 8, 14
European Union, 13, 17, 26, 28, 33, 49, 59, 61, 82

## F

Fibonacci, 138

## I

'Fibonacci', 139

## F

Finland, 11, 13, 15, 75, 82, 83, 85, 86, 87, 91, 95, 115, 127, 150
France, 7, 34, 38, 68
Frederick II the Great, 8
Frondizi, 113

## G

Germany, 10, 32, 33, 34, 37, 38, 39, 49, 53, 73, 82, 107, 115, 150
Gini, 74
Goh Chok Tong, 42
Great Britain, 20

## H

Hong Kong, 10, 22, 74

## I

Iceland, 10, 13, 26, 67
India, 22
Individual taxpayer, 79
Indonesia, 22
Israel, 11, 67

## J

Japan, 11, 20, 22, 73
Jean Jacques Rousseau, 7
John Locke, 7

## K

Kenya, 38

## L

Latin America, 6, 7, 9, 17, 96, 107, 114
Lee Hsien Loong, 42
Lee Kuan Yew, 42, 146, 155
Liechtenstein, 11, 26
Lucius Clay, 34
Ludwing Erhard, 34
Lutheran, 8, 14, 84
Luxembourg, 49

## M

Macondo, 105
Mads Mikkelsen, 49
Malaysia, 22
Martin Luther, 8
Max Weber, 36
Menzies, Sir Robert, 19

Mexico, 92
Milton Friedman, 118, 137, 146

## N

NAFTA, 67
Netherlands, 38, 49, 62, 82
New Zealand, 10, 15, 22, 53, 88
Nordic countries, 5, 14, 82, 92, 111, 144
North Korea, 73
Noruega, 10
Norway, 12, 13, 15, 16, 17, 18, 26, 31, 49, 53, 62, 67, 86, 90, 115, 151, 153, 155, 162

## O

OECD, 5, 16, 21, 22, 23, 28, 29, 36, 49, 50, 51, 67, 70, 76, 79, 81, 85, 92, 95, 97, 111, 118, 120, 121, 122, 126, 129, 157, 158, 159

## P

Park Chun Hee, 73
Pasi Sahlberg, 86
Peru, 22, 67, 92
PISA, 22, 29, 30, 36, 60, 68, 76, 85, 86, 92, 119, 120, 121, 160
Prussia, 8
PyMEs, 79

## R

*Reconquista*, 9
Russia, 33, 82, 83

## S

Sarmiento, 112
Saudi Arabia, 65
Seán Lemass, 59, 61
Singapore, 5, 10, 40, 41, 44, 45, 46, 47, 53, 68, 73, 74, 91, 97, 98, 115, 130, 145, 152, 155, 161, 162, 164
Sir Robert Menzies, 20
SMEs, 15, 141, 142
South Korea, 11, 20, 73, 74, 76, 78, 91, 111, 115
St. Patrick, 57
Sweden, 10, 13, 15, 49, 53, 62, 82, 117, 118, 119, 120, 122, 146, 157
Switzerland, 10, 25, 26, 28, 29, 30, 49, 67, 90, 98, 111, 115, 147, 154, 159

## T

TIMSS, 22, 44

## U

United Nations, 10, 26, 49, 154
United States, 7, 17, 20, 22, 29, 34, 38, 49, 51, 58, 65, 69, 86, 98, 159
Uruguay, 92
USSR, 73

## V

Venezuela, 65, 135
Viking, 13

## W

World Bank, 15, 53, 74, 164
World War II, 20, 33, 73, 83, 111

www.ingramcontent.com/pod-product-compliance
Lightning Source LLC
Chambersburg PA
CBHW021411210526
45463CB00001B/325